9^{30}

FIC   Garfield, Leon
GAR
          The golden shadow

DATE			
MAR 20 92			

The Golden Shadow

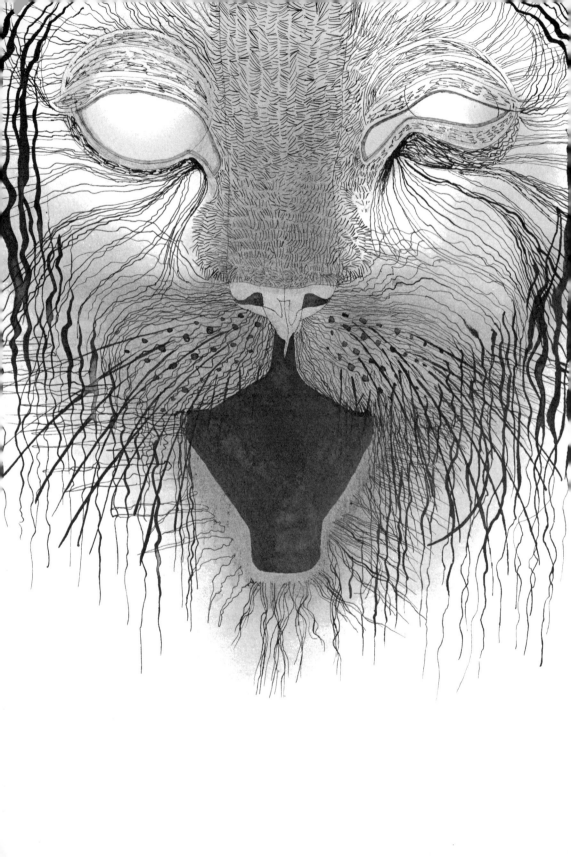

The Golden Shadow

●

Leon Garfield
&
Edward Blishen

Illustrated by Charles Keeping

●

Pantheon Books

Library of Congress Cataloging in Publication Data

Garfield, Leon.
The golden shadow.
SUMMARY: Retells in a continuous narrative the activities and
adventures of the Greek gods and goddesses and their
relationships with each other and with human beings.
[1. Mythology, Greek]   I. Blishen, Edward, 1920- joint author.
II. Keeping, Charles, illus.   III. Title
PZ7.G17943Gp   [Fic]   73-1402
ISBN 0-394-82704-X   ISBN 0-394-92704-4 (lib. bdg.)

Contents

To
Vivien,
Nancy
and
Renate

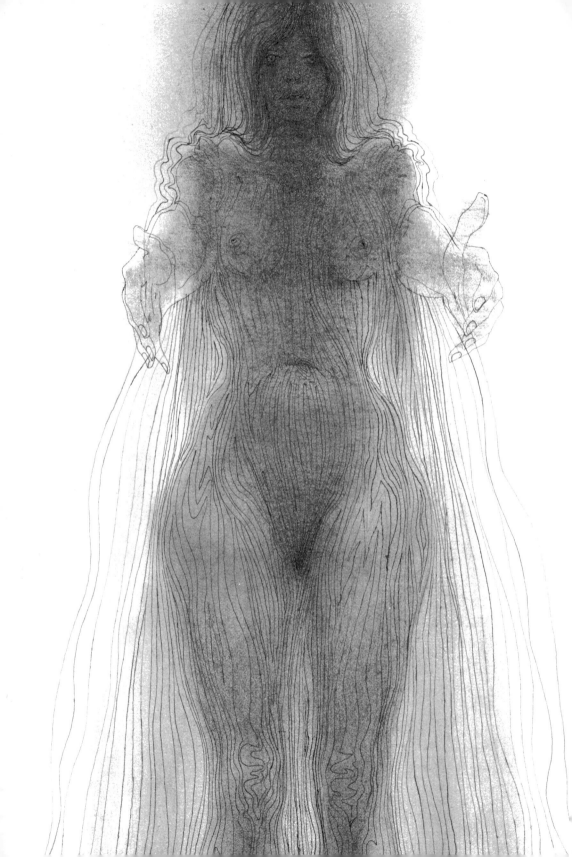

1 ● The Prophecy

It began one morning in Thessaly when a young fisherman strolled across the sands. Ahead stood a promontory of rocks beyond which lay his boat. With a practised eye he looked out to sea and nodded; it would be a prosperous morning. Then, as he curved his steps to match the curving of the incoming tide, the rising sun struck him full in the face and dissolved sea, sky and land into a blaze of orange, silver and gold. He hastened onward to reach the shadow of the rocks; when suddenly he heard the sound of a woman's voice. He stopped. The voice was low and gentle and wonderfully sweet. Ordinarily he was of an open, simple disposition; eavesdropping was remote from his nature. But an air of secrecy seemed to have been enjoined upon him; in spite of himself he held his breath and listened.

The words he overheard were widely spaced—as if the speaker had all the time in the world to ask her haunting question:

"Tell me—tell me, who will my lover be?"

A smile caught the corners of the fisherman's lips; cautiously he crept towards a narrow cleft in the rocks and began to insinuate himself through. This cleft turned sharply before opening out onto the sands beyond. In the angle of the turn, he paused.

Not far from where his scarlet-painted boat lay kissing its shadow by the water's edge, he saw two seated figures. One crouched on the sands with her knees drawn up to her chin. She wore a fine-spun robe of blue that fell away from her ankles, revealing bright sandals fashioned out of silver in the shape of ferns. He could not see her face; all but the curve of her cheek was obscured by the dark torrent of her hair.

The second figure was also that of a woman, but old—old and grave and still as the sea-worn stone on which she sat. Her gown was grey and caught in by a girdle of linked bronze. Beside her, carelessly tumbled in the sand, lay a pair of wooden scales such as a careful housekeeper might have used to weigh out herbs; but the old woman did not look like a housekeeper. There was an air of threatening grandeur about her that frightened the young fisherman.

Again he heard the age-old question asked—even as any warm girl might have asked her grandmother in the corner of a harvest field:

"Tell me, who will my lover be?"

The old woman moved. She reached down to grasp her scales, when the other interposed a white hand as if unwilling to take what the scales might bring.

"Then no more than this," murmured the old woman, leaving the scales untouched. "You will bear a son who will be greater than his father. Does it please you?" Her voice was monotonous and flat, inclining neither to pleasure nor distress. "Is it enough to know?"

"Yes . . . yes. It is enough, great lady. . . ."

The old woman nodded and rose; she tucked her scales in the girdle of her gown and trudged away across the sands towards the lifting sun. Unable to continue looking, the fisherman lowered his eyes and stared down at her footprints until the sea whispered over them and washed them away. When he looked again, the old woman had gone.

But the other, the woman in blue, still remained crouching and gazing over the bright nothingness of the sea. Her gown clung closely about her, and her soft flesh shone through.

The fisherman's heart beat furiously and he began to force his way through the cleft. Perhaps already in his thoughts were the tales he'd be able to tell of his grand adventure by the sea—of the catch he'd made on the sands far better than any he'd got in the sea.

He stumbled out of the sharp rocks and stood, golden in the sunshine; a very handsome young man and well knowing it.

"Lady," he said softly, but not without pride, "I'll be your lover and give you that son who'll turn out even grander than me."

He waited, beaming confidently; he couldn't for the life of him see any reason to be otherwise. Slowly the woman rose; then she turned and smiled at him.

He caught no more than a glimpse of her face; she had moved so that she stood directly between him and the sun and so was in the deepest shadow. His knees shook and sweat began to trickle down his back, stinging his flesh where it had been scraped by the rocks. Her face had been beautiful enough almost to make him cry; and her smile had been one of fathomless contempt.

The young man's innocent eyes filled with tears of humiliation. Unable to move he stared at her while the sun blazed through her gown in every particular, turning it into a faint blue mist about her naked body. She opened her arms as if to invite him.

"A son," she laughed softly, "even greater than you?"

She moved her head and the sudden blinding light made the fisherman shut his eyes in pain. He heard her laugh again, mockingly; and when he opened his eyes she, like the grave old woman with the scales, was gone.

"Lady, lady!" shouted the fisherman, frightened and dismayed. "Come back to me!"

He ran up and down the sands, calling wildly; but no one answered, no one came. He remained there for two hours or more, lying beside his boat, weeping inexplicably into the warm sand. Then he climbed into his boat and sat there, with his chin in his hands and staring out to sea. There was an ache in his chest and he believed his heart had been broken.

At last other fishermen came to see what had become of him. Mournfully he told them of his adventure and of the marvellous catch that had got away. But they, being fishermen too, smiled knowingly and laid their heads on one side.

At this, the young man grew angry; fisherman though he was, he was still telling the truth. So his friends shrugged their shoulders and left him to his fantastic dreams. Time would cure him. . . .

But time did not cure him. Instead he told his story over and over again till all Thessaly must have heard it. Even travellers passing through were plucked aside and forced to listen while they took refreshment. No one was spared the young man's story; and after each telling, the fisherman—now no longer quite so young—would look at his listener pleadingly and say:

"Who do you think she was?" He had truly fallen in love with his vision, and on brilliant mornings he would still go down to the haunted stretch of sand and call and search and listen for the lady who longed for a lover but would not have him.

Then, one evening, there came to his village a traveller more willing to listen than the rest. This traveller, bald and short of sight, was a poet, a storyteller, who collected tales that he wove into ballads for the entertainment of any who'd clothe and feed him.

The fisherman's adventure fascinated him. He asked to hear it twice over. Immensely flattered, the fisherman obliged; and finished, as usual, with his hopeless question. "Who do you think she was?"

The storyteller smiled. Plainly he was in two minds. Which one should he offer?

"My friend," he said quietly, but avoiding the fisherman's eyes. "I can promise nothing, but I think you might have seen immortals. It is possible, just possible, that the lady of the silver sandals was Thetis, the sea goddess, who once nursed the infant Hephaestus in a grotto under the sea. He made her such a pair of sandals when first he tried his hand at metalwork. I envy you for having seen them; they must have been wonderful to behold."

"And—and the other?" cried the fisherman, tremendously excited by such news.

The storyteller frowned, as if suddenly doubting himself. "The scales . . . yes, the scales." He hesitated, and a chill entered the little cottage where they sat. "You have described Themis, sister of the Titans and mother of the Fates. It seems you saw the goddess of Order, my friend, and heard her prophesy; though what was meant by it, none of us can say."

"That Thetis's son will be more handsome than his father," repeated the fisherman.

"I thought she said 'greater'."

"It's the same," said the fisherman, who could imagine nothing more powerful than good looks.

The storyteller smiled and patted the fisherman's stout arm; then he departed, leaving the fisherman contented at last that he'd lost his heart to a goddess who, in the nature of things, had refused him for no worse reason than his being merely a man.

The travelling storyteller went his ways, picking up more and more scraps to fill out his most ambitious tale of the births and doings of the Olympian gods. Patterns fell into place, the Seasons explained themselves, famines and disasters stood revealed; but nowhere could he fit in the mysterious prophecy of Themis to the Lady of the Sea. So he was reduced to telling it, with a loud flourish on his lyre, quite on its own—as an extra item— when the main body of his tale was done and his audience was plainly expecting more.

He journeyed from fireside to fireside, staring short-sightedly into the changing castles in the crumbling flames, and ever weaving his way northward. Through the bronze-floored halls of palaces and mansions he passed, never remaining anywhere longer than a single night. It was as if the Fates were driving him in this one direction, and, at times, it pleased him to think so. But truth to tell, there were other reasons. Men in the north, though rougher, were more generous and had not heard his tales before.

He passed through Macedonia, then Thrace, until he came to Salmydessus where he embarked in a stout painted galley bound for Colchis with a cargo of dyed wool. The merchant who owned the vessel was glad enough of the storyteller, as the voyage was long and such a passenger would soothe the tedious evenings and engross the restive crew.

Nightly when the great sail was furled and a sea-anchor put out, a brazier of wrought-iron was carried into the shelter of the high stern; a fire was lit and all gathered round, wrapped in woollen cloaks (for the nights were bitter cold), to listen to the storyteller earn his keep. "At first," he would begin, with a rapid flourish on his lyre, "it was no more than a tiny prick of light against the immense blue fabric of the sky . . ." and he would go on to tell of the world's beginning and the birth of the gods. . . . Eagerly the sailors hung on his words, sharply silencing any skinny critic who'd heard it all before but differently told, until in the fireglow their wide eyes and mouths agape made a honeycomb of wonderment.

On and on the galley voyaged, until thick grey mists began to roll across the sea, obscuring sky and water for hours at a time. Steering became hazardous and soundings were taken uneasily— for there was often a smell in the air of mountainous land. Sometimes by day sea-birds were heard screaming, but they were never seen; the sailors rested on their oars and grew pale for fear of nearby rocks. Once, and only once, a bird was seen, through a brief cleft in the mist. It looked to be a bird of prey with curved beak and huge, powerful wings whose quill feathers rose and fell like the oars of a flying galley. It vanished almost directly, and the storyteller stared into the thick sky till his short-sighted eyes ran over with tears of strain.

One night two anchors were put out, for the mists were heavy and the smell of land strong. The fire spat and crackled, then settled down to a steady burning that turned the hollow of the high stern into a tall ribbed shrine, full of jostling shadows and whispers of expectation.

The storyteller, with a quick, upward glance, plucked his lyre, and the single notes sang out like arrows from the strings, and penetrated the recesses of the night. He began to tell of the making of man by the Titan Prometheus, and of how he stole fire from heaven for his shivering creatures; and then how Zeus punished him most hideously for his charitable crime. "Far, far to the north, amid the frozen mountains of the Caucasus, there stood a pillar. Here the naked Titan was manacled by ankles and wrists, while an eternal vulture tore at his undefended liver till the anger of Zeus should be appeased. Such was the punishment of Prometheus, maker of men."

The storyteller's voice died away, and all leaned forward to catch his slightest whisper. Suddenly the fire in the brazier leaped, as a charred piece of wood burned through with a flurry of sparks. The storyteller started; he looked upward, then the fire quietened and all about the ship there was no sound but the black water muttering as it made little glinting snakes about the nodding prow.

"Tell us another tale," murmured a voice from the shadows, "for this seems the longest night in the world."

The storyteller smiled ruefully; he'd all but exhausted his stock.

"I'll tell you a tale of a strange prophesy by a sea-shore," he said wearily; "but who can say what it means, or who it concerns, or even why I should tell it here and now? Once in Thessaly, a young fisherman walked along the early morning sands. . . ."

As he spoke, a breeze sprang up and began to agitate the mists into deep passages and sudden hollows; but the storyteller had become absorbed in his story of the curious promise concerning Thetis's child. He saw nothing of what was in the air about him; and at first scarcely heard the look-out's cry from the prow of "Land! Land! Beware!"

The mists had parted in a huge place, and fallen back like the breached ruins of some enormous wall. Rocks and mountains loomed beyond; tremendous pilings-up of boulders that glinted with far-off ice. Here and there wound white torrents, frozen in the very act of rushing down to the black sea.

"What's that? What is it?" shouted the look-out. "High up, over there!"

He pointed fearfully towards a weird configuration of distant rock that seemed to move and twist as the vapours coiled and spread. Then the mists returned in force and all was hidden from sight.

"Didn't you see it?" the look-out asked the bald old story-teller who kept plaguing him to say exactly, precisely how and what he'd seen.

"It looked so much alive . . . only so tall and huge. It seemed to move, you know, almost as if it was chained to something. Didn't you see it at all?"

"A mark! Was there a mark—a wound in its side?"

"Who could say from so far off? It might have been nothing more than a queer old cliff, shifting under its weight of ice. Didn't you see it?"

"My eyes are not so sharp as yours," said the storyteller sadly. "I saw only—rocks. And yet, I felt that. . . ."

"Then rocks it was," said the look-out, with a sudden rush of compassion for the dejected storyteller. In his heart of hearts he knew that what he'd glimpsed, slowly writhing amid the distant mountainous ice, had been something the storyteller had set great store on; would have given his cracked old eyes to have seen; might even have given his life itself for. So he settled for a tall cliff that, for an instant, had looked like a gigantic figure, chained by ankle and wrist, and bleeding from its side. Hollows filled with ice had glinted down on the anchored galley—not eyes.

The storyteller smiled sadly, and understood. Though he sang every night of gods and immortals, filled his mind with them and was more familiar with their ways than with his own, he himself had never glimpsed so much as a Nereid—at least, not that he could take his oath on. Yet a simple fisherman had seen Themis and silver-sandalled Thetis; and a humble sailor had actually beheld—

Fiercely he called his thoughts to order, and brushed aside the tears that streamed from his useless eyes. The pursuit of knowledge had blinded him. He had lost the power to behold the divine; and worse, almost the strength to believe in it.

"Prometheus!" he wept. "Great Prometheus, why did I come? Was it only to break my own heart? Why did *I* not see you?"

2 • A Strange Affair at Thebes

The night continued; one by one the sailors on the anchored galley drowsed away, some wrapped in their cloaks while others, creeping among the baled-up cargo of wool, coiled like children fallen asleep while playing in a giant's bed. The storyteller slept with his bald head pressed against the mast and glinting in the faint starlight like a wrinkled egg of secrets.

The woods were quiet, the seas rustled dreamily under the sky.

On the isle of Aegina, the palace, ordinarily so noisy with the clatter and shrieks of children, was quiet; the three infants, Telamon, Peleus and tiny Phorcus, lay tangled in each other's arms, unknowing that one day, not very far off, two of the brothers would murder the third who now smiled blindly between them in one sleep.

From Crete to the Caucasus and then beyond, the tide of night flowed on, drowning the world in dreams. The painted galley lay anchored in the Caucasian fogs, even though the storyteller's fire had long since died and turned to feathery white.

Huge eyes, full of ice and pity, looked down on the little vessel and observed the storyteller's faintly gleaming head. Lips, fissured and cracked like the surrounding rock, moved in a compassionate smile; the toppling cliff, the weird configuration of crags that had frightened the look-out, stirred slowly—so as not to chafe the rawness caused by chains.

Already the wound in the side had healed; Prometheus the Titan waited for the morning that would bring the vulture to tear at him again. Wearily he turned towards the east; the waiting for day was worse than the pain it would bring. The night seemed to have continued far beyond its natural limit. Zeus, his enemy, was abroad; the Titan knew it.

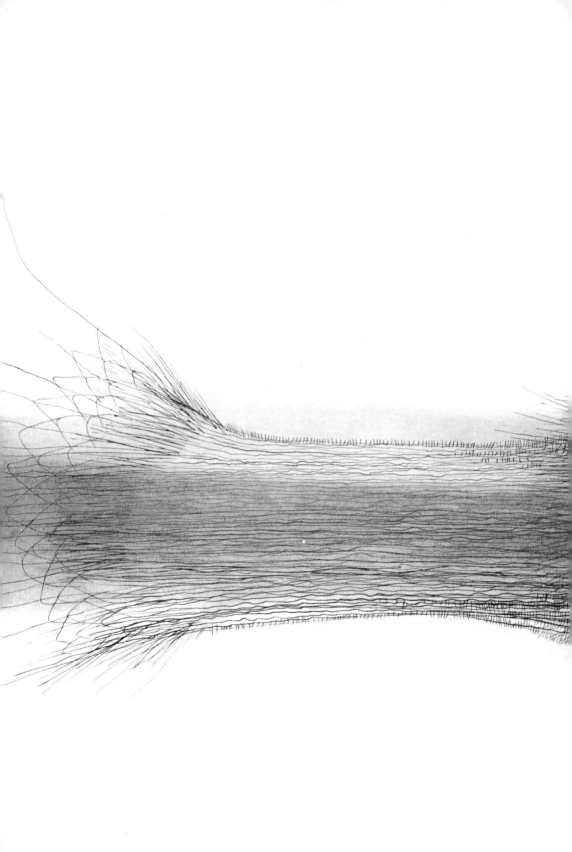

Through what door or window, and in what dark town, Prometheus wondered, was coming the deceiving bird, or golden shower, or cloud of black to set the dogs whimpering and the woman within panting with desire?

Was the god in Thessaly? The prophecy of Themis, that had drifted up to him from the painted galley, echoed in his thoughts. Was Thetis still crouching by the sea, waiting for the lover who would beget the longed-for child?

Would her lover be Zeus? Was this the very night when Zeus would at last sow the seed of his own destruction and beget a child greater than himself?

Prometheus dreamed of being freed by such a child; he looked up to the stars; one by one they went out as if unwilling to betray the present whereabouts of Zeus.

The darkness was now almost absolute; the blind prophet Teiresias who woke briefly, thought himself still asleep; and on the battlefield outside Oechalia, camp sentries snored beside watch-fires that had dwindled to pin-prick eyes. Even the sharp-eyed robbers yawned and dozed beside the half-stripped bodies of the newly dead; and in his unguarded tent Amphitryon, the victorious commander, dreamed of Alcmena, his wife in distant Thebes—and of the love-making when he should return; for Alcmena's hot beauty was such as might have aroused even a god. . . .

"Amphitryon—oh! Amphitryon!" moaned Alcmena, deep in the royal bed of Thebes; and the Amphitryon beside her laughed, hid his strangely golden eyes—and enjoyed her yet again.

But silver-sandalled Thetis crouched on the shore in Thessaly, still dreaming of an unknown lover and an unborn son; she was alone.

At last the darkness faded and withered before the dawn. The huge bird of prey whose quill feathers rose and fell like banked oars, flew once more over the painted galley and vanished into the retreating mists. Soon the storyteller heard it shriek among the echoing rocks; he knew it must be the cry of the bird—for what else was there so high up in the rifting ice? But the sailors trembled that anything could scream so long and loud as to shake the vessel from prow to stern and rattle the sail like a dried skin.

That same day they came to Colchis where the storyteller stayed for no more than his customary single night. The tall buildings of the palace were shut against him; the queen was in labour and no one had a mind for ballads. Later he heard that a daughter had been born whose name was Medea, and that goddesses had been on hand. He smiled, a shade sardonically; they were always in the last town, or the next one; never before his eyes. Yet whenever he sang of them he truly believed; and when he finished, he was half envious and half glad to see his beliefs survive his song, even if only in other hearts than his own. If only—ah! if only his sight had been as keen as the look-out's or the fisherman's on the Thessalian shore!

Even the tale of Themis's prophecy to the sea-goddess, which had made such a mark on him at the time, seemed altogether dream-like now—as the world aged. Nonetheless, he continued to tell it; he had his living to earn. Once more he turned his steps southward and journeyed slowly from fireside to fireside, picking up scraps to extend the scope of his tale; and always hoping, against reasons that mounted up like cold stone walls, that one day he would come upon one single piece of proof that would put his doubts to flight. As he trudged the blinding roads, he turned his head from side to side with an eager, desperate smile—as if any moment his short-sighted eyes would at last see a god.

On the low hills north of the valley of the river Asopus stands Thebes, city of the seven gates. Cadmus built it, with the help of men who sprang, plumed like corn, from a furrow sown with a serpent's teeth. This furrow, much grassed over, was still preserved; but the men of Thebes looked no more supernatural in their origins than the rest of mankind to the storyteller as he trudged through the meanest of the seven gates.

As was his custom he made first for the servants' quarters of the palace, to discover the master's mood and temper, and also to gather crumbs of gossip such as he might weave flatteringly into his nightly song. This was the subtlest part of the storyteller's art—to lace his wonders with the homely touch of local talk. Although he was always pleased to hear staid housekeepers' tales of recent visits from the gods, kitchen maids' scandals of the spicier doings of men fascinated him quite as much.

No sooner had he entered the servants' hall and washed the dust and sand from his hard broad feet than he learned that the lord Amphitryon and pious Alcmena were estranged. The great man had not entered her bed since the day he'd returned from the bloody field of Oechalia, full of his soldierly triumphs. A sly, witty serving-girl almost killed herself with laughing as she confided how Amphitryon had come home, eager to boast of his exploits in the war. But the virtuous lady Alcmena had yawned and said:

"Not again, my lord. Between love-makings last night I heard how every single javelin found its mark, whose armour it pierced, and which warrior was engulfed by hateful night. But perhaps tomorrow, my lord, you shall tell it to me all over again."

"But who told you?" cried Amphitryon, entirely amazed.

"Why, you did, my lord—in bed, last night. Have you forgotten?"

Then the lord Amphitryon flew into the most dreadful rage as he understood some scoundrel had forestalled him and, under cover of the famous long night, had filled his place and even stolen the thunder of his warrior's tale.

"And since that time," laughed the serving-girl, "he's not gone near her! I fancy he's been afraid to show up badly beside that other Amphitryon who, from all accounts, must have been quite a man!"

Then the housekeeper, more staid than most, overheard the laughter and sent the girl packing with a box on her ears, and proceeded to set the storyteller to rights.

"It was almighty Zeus himself," she explained, somewhat grandly—for she respected her royal lord and lady second only to the gods, "who came to my lady that night in her husband's shape, to beget a son upon her who would rule the House of Perseus."

The storyteller nodded—and strove to avoid the serving-girl's mocking eyes.

"But the goddess Hera was jealous of my lady who'd unknowingly become great Zeus's queen for a night," went on the housekeeper carefully. "Else how do you explain why sickly little Eurystheus was born a seven months child to the vain queen of

Mycenae if not to forestall our own sweet baby here by a single fatal day? This was Hera's work, my friend. And, meaning no disrespect to the lord Amphitryon, anyone can see, with half an eye, that our Heracles is a son of Zeus."

Here the serving-girl shut one eye, covered half the other and put on such a look of admiring awe that the storyteller could scarcely keep his face respectfully straight.

There was no doubt that the lord Amphitryon was not particularly prepossessing; he was shortish, with greasy black hair and eyes of a muddy grey. His high birth showed more in his manner than in his aspect. But Alcmena was lovely almost beyond compare. Perhaps her chin was not so firm as some, and her nose not so fine as might be, but these imperfections gave her a ripe and tender humanity that caught at the heart and made it ache. Side by side they sat—with a tell-tale space between them—and prepared to listen to the storyteller's song.

The fire in the hearth burned smoothly; the castles within it were all domestic. Whatever gods had once walked in Thebes, only shrewd and fanciful mankind dwelt there now. The storyteller, wondering how best he might introduce the housekeeper's tale of Zeus's night of love and the marvellous child he'd begotten on Alcmena, scratched his head. Then he raised his hand to pluck his lyre.

He paused. A sudden chill had swept through the marble-floored hall. The fire leaped—and sent frightened shadows flying up the pillars to hide themselves trembling under the dark roof; and in the stillness a curious rustling was heard—a dry, scraping sound that passed from one side of the hall to the other.

All movement, all whispering of gowns, easing of limbs, all breathing, even, seemed to have ceased; the storyteller frowned as he observed his own upraised hand trembling violently. Presently the intrusive rustling sound was heard no more; but the chill remained, and so did the stillness. Then the silence was broken. From somewhere in the palace came the sound of a woman screaming; and of a child laughing.

3 • Snakes in the Nursery

A strange, sweetish smell pervaded the nursery; it came from a light that had poured in quite suddenly—like a heavy golden mist—from between the carved capitals of the pillars that flanked the door. In a corner of the room, attempting to shield her eyes against the light, which tickled and stung her withered skin, crouched an old woman, a nurse. It was she who had screamed; but now, though her mouth still gaped, she was unable to utter more than a faint irregular gasping.

In the middle of the room stood a cot with shield-shaped sides in which a naked child of some ten months was standing upright. He had flung out his lamb's wool fleece which lay tumbled over the end of the cot. He was chuckling and laughing and beckoning with fat, dimpled hands towards something on the floor, first on one side and then on the other. As he beckoned, the dry rustling, heard previously in the hall, began again; the nurse renewed her efforts to scream.

The rustling ceased; and two huge snakes—whose steady writhing motion across the marble floors had produced the arresting sound—began to twist and nuzzle upward towards the child's eager hands. The flat, venomous heads moved uncertainly back and forth as if seeking a purchase on the carved wood; then they lifted up to a level with the child's neck where they remained, swaying slightly and tasting the misty golden air with rapid black tongues.

A sound of footsteps momentarily halted the swaying heads. The light in the room began to dwindle rapidly and had vanished almost entirely by the time the door was flung open and torchlight crowded in.

Alcmena and Aphitryon stood just within the doorway as if turned to stone. They had seen the poised snakes and dared not move for fear of distracting them into striking the child. Then little Heracles, delighted by an audience, reached out inquisitively and began to finger the scaly heads whose cold eyes were fixed on certain portions of his neck.

Alcmena moaned; the child had grasped the serpents at the base of their heads so that their jaws gaped and venom dribbled from their fangs. Then he began to play with them, but never releasing his hold. He drew the terrible heads together as if to kiss them, then jerked them rapidly apart. Their enormous coils began to boil up on either side of the cot until, like a stirring of bronze, they poured over the edge to engulf the child within.

Fascinated, he tried to stand on them, even to play with them with his feet, until he seemed to lose patience and grow angry. He scowled from gaping head to head as if puzzling which led to which distracted tail; for he stood now, chest-high in a writhing turmoil that had neither beginning nor end. Suddenly all motion stopped; the coils shuddered and grew still. The child's frowns vanished; he smiled and let go of the snakes' heads which dropped like broken toys. He had strangled them.

The mother and father waited till morning, for the man they needed was perilously old and every hour of sleep most necessary to him; then they summoned Teiresias, the blind seer of Thebes. They told him everything, and waited impatiently on his reply; the man was so old that his tongue seemed to have withered in his mouth. Some said it was the goddess Athene who had blinded him for seeing her in her bath, while others declared he'd lost his eyes by Hera's hand for giving judgement against her in a dispute with almighty Zeus. But it had been so many years ago that Teiresias himself could no longer be certain and told sometimes one tale and sometimes the other. Either way, it had been a goddess who'd done it; and either way, she had given him eyes within in place of those he'd lost without.

Supported by servants, the seer listened first to the nurse, then to Amphitryon and lastly to Alcmena herself. He commanded the dead reptiles to be fetched—and monstrous creatures they turned out to be in the light of day—twice as long as a man and thick, at their greatest part, as Amphytrion's powerful thigh. The blind man laid his hands on them, felt their scales and asked of their colour, which, though now a flabby grey, had been in life a cold malignant blue.

"Heracles has a mighty enemy," he said at length. "These serpents were sent by Hera herself to destroy him. Yet somehow Zeus has protected him. The child will be a great hero, lady Alcmena; perhaps the greatest of all; but Hera's enmity will always pursue him. She will send other destroyers, even serpents of the mind."

Alcmena shuddered; but Amphitryon, thinking only of the glory, smiled.

"Wise Teiresias," said the staid housekeeper, who was a woman of much country wisdom and magical herbs. "What shall we do with the serpents, and what herbs should we strew in the doorways to protect this house?"

Teiresias frowned; he was no lover of superstition.

"If I were you," he said dryly, "I would burn the snakes before they begin to rot; and I would strew such herbs as would take off the edge of the stink."

He was carried from the palace and nodded as he felt the bright sun.

"Let me walk," he mumbled to his servants; and they gave him two staffs of wild olive and tenderly watched him creep across the courtyard towards the gate.

A figure emerged from the shadows of the outer wall. He was bald and weathered-looking, with worn garments and screwed-up eyes; he carried a lyre. . . .

"Teiresias," murmured the storyteller, and laid his hand on the blind man's sleeve. Having been left at the fireside during the commotion of the night, and forgotten during the excitement of the morning, he'd lingered in the hope of speaking with the famous prophet who, as the world knew, had seen and talked with the gods themselves.

"Tell me about the gods," he breathed. "Tell me what they are really like."

Teiresias smiled; he sensed the world of anguished pleading behind the stranger's question; he divined the man who longed for proof—yet would helplessly destroy it even as he found it.

"They resemble men," he said gently; "and when you behold

one of them it is as if you have come face to face with some famous statue after having known it only from a thousand clumsy copies. For men are but poor imitations in a grosser substance, my friend. The gods shine, so that it is not easy to observe their exact outlines; there is a sense of flowing. Great Hera moves continually; even her dark hair seems always flying. The lady Athene is restless, too, though her movements are more measured. I saw divine Hephaestus; his golden skin is all pitted and burnt by sparks from his forge, and he still smells of the sea. He moves on golden leg-supports, but is very sure and quick."

"And Almighty Zeus?"

"I saw only his back, my friend, and it was like a shining mountain. He was with Hermes, who looked quite small and slight; he was more silvery than the others. His face was smiling and his eyes looked sideways, as if at some joke that only he had seen. I would not trust Hermes; and yet he is the god we must all, sooner or later, take by the hand."

The storyteller listened, at first awed, then filled with doubt. The man was so old. . . . Had he ever seen?

"Who was it who blinded you, Teiresias? Was it the lady Hera or—?"

"I forget," mumbled Teiresias, worn out with talking. "It was so long—so very long ago."

Do you remember *anything*, thought the storyteller, or have you been blind from birth? So, to test the prophet, he asked him about the sea and what colour it reminded him of; for only a man who has once seen can comprehend what colour is.

"Dark," said Teiresias, frowningly. "Dark, like wine."

The storyteller sighed; this was the answer of a man who had never possessed eyes. The gods and goddesses he'd seen had all been inside his head. So the storyteller trudged away still seeking, with screwed-up eyes and questing mind, what he knew, in his heart of hearts, he would never find.

Soon seven-gated Thebes disappeared in the dust behind him; and with it, the infant Heracles, son of Zeus, whom the goddess Hera had sworn to destroy.

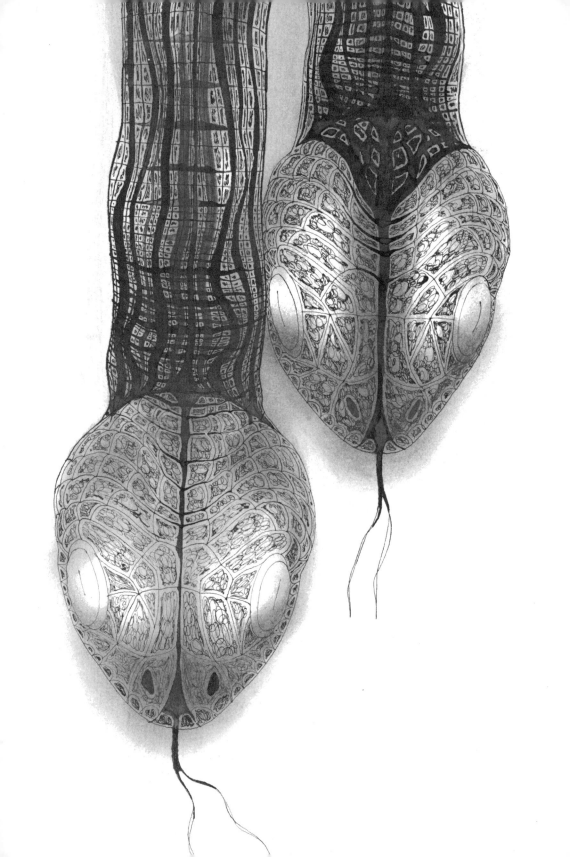

4 • Snakes in the Mind

Hera, wife of Zeus, wove her serpentine web of revenge; but now she played with little snakes as thin as air, loosing them to bore into eyes, ears and nostrils and sting the vulnerable brain within. Down, down, down they wriggled, spitting like a warm rain. . . .

On the isle of Aegina three children who once had shared the same cot, were already half way to glory. Telamon and Peleus were sturdy and handsome enough; but Phorcus, the youngest, eclipsed them with dazzling ease. He was the golden apple of his father's eye; even Chiron, the Centaur, applauded his skill when, with his brothers, he attended the famous school on Mount Pelion where the Centaur had his cave. Half horse, half man, and uniting the best of both creatures, Chiron was very ancient in his origins and a leader of his race. His cave was crammed with lyres, swords and instruments of astronomy, so that his pupils often complained that there was nowhere to sit down except on the Centaur's broad back. Nonetheless, it was here that the world's princes came to learn the last refinements of the arts of peace and war from one who was a master of them all. They were indeed a splendid band of youths; they came to Chiron only when they had surpassed all their masters at home.

Heracles of Thebes longed to join them, and was more than ready. Amphitryon himself had taught him to drive a chariot, and when the boy took the reins the horses leaped as if for the first time they knew a master's hand. So it was with everything; his tutors, excellent as they were, could only smile ruefully as the gifted child passed them by. But unluckily there was one art in which he lagged behind: literature. He had Linus for his teacher . . . who, though the son of an easy-running river god, was a most obstinate and pedantic man. So Heracles remained in Thebes until such time as Linus should declare himself surpassed. But this Linus could never do; his head was stuffed with rusty rules that, in the poor light, he took for gold, so the pupil was wilful, backward and blind who failed to submit to the self-same shackles that imprisoned Linus himself.

Now it happened once, on a fine warm day with no prospect of rain, that Heracles looked forward to a pleasant morning by the river where the Theban girls washed out their fathers' robes. His music master was ill—as often happened in fine weather when there were nymphs about—so the boy dutifully unhooked his lyre from the schoolroom wall and set out for some serenading of a practical kind.

"And where do you think you are going?"

Linus stood before him, his glum face screwed up against the sun as if offended by it. Heracles began to explain when Linus held up his hand. He knew music; he would hear the lesson in the absent master's place. There would be no outdoor serenading, no matter how sweetly shone the day. The boy sighed; but being well-tutored in philosophy, he knew the art of being resigned.

"Ah, well," he said, retreating into the dark schoolroom, "it is coming on to rain, anyway."

Linus frowned. "I think not."

Heracles shrugged his broad shoulders. He did not want to contradict, but he had felt, quite distinctly, on his forehead and eyelids several drops of warmish rain.

Linus mounted the stone rostrum and laid his ugly hands on the engraved bronze rail. "Play me," he said, indicating the rough wooden pupil's stool, "the exercise you have been instructed to prepare."

Heracles put his foot on the stool and cradled his lyre on his thigh. He glanced out to the sunshine and blinked fiercely; his eyes were quite wet—perhaps with regret over the lively Theban girls by the river; or perhaps from some sudden dream of that band of graceful youths at Chiron's cave on Mount Pelion where he, the best of them all, could never go. Or perhaps the wetness was no more than from the spots of warm rain that had fallen so unaccountably from the radiant sky.

He began to play, not an exercise, but a piece of his own invention. He did this because he longed passionately to show Linus that the spirit of fancy had not been crushed in him; also

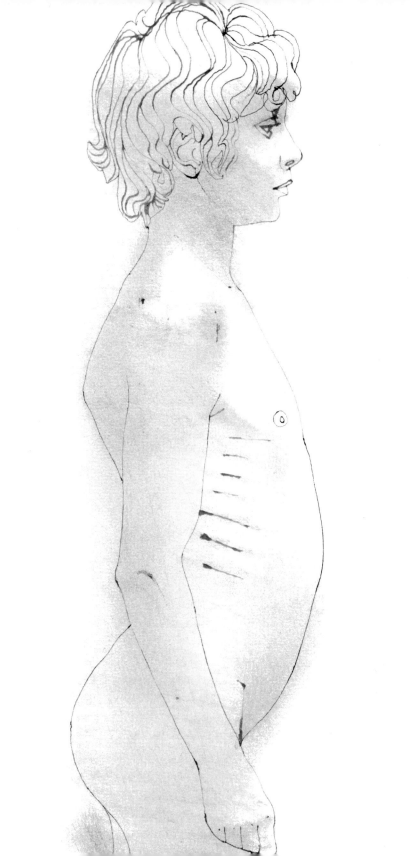

he honestly desired to please and impress the man.

With powerful and strikingly dexterous fingers, he began upon a loud, rapid passage in which the notes tumbled helter-skelter as if down a flight of steps. Then before the echoes of this singing uproar had died from the room, he bent his head low as if to catch the single notes of a solemn measure he plucked from his instrument. Somehow this measure, in its very dignity, seemed a mischievous parody of the heavy-footed walk of Linus himself, for, every now and then, it would hurry, as Linus himself did when he thought no one was looking. Linus compressed his lips; and when this ponderous measure turned out to be no more than the accompaniment of a grandly dancing tune, he felt the mockery in it and his eyes glittered with anger.

Heracles played on, embroidering his themes with all the wit, grandeur and beauty he could command. His fingers, multiplied by speed, transfigured the strings into a vibrating mist of gold—like some great dragon-fly's wing; until, with a sudden flick, he arrested all sound and motion. He smiled, almost laughed—and with a second cascade of notes even mightier than

the first, he brought his piece to a humorously triumphant end. He looked up; he knew he had never played better in his life.

"You play," said Linus evenly, "as if with the hooves of a boar."

"And you listen," replied Heracles furiously, "as if with the ears of an ass!"

Linus flushed; never before had he been answered back. He left the rostrum, snatched the lyre and struck the insolent pupil heavily across the shoulders with it. Tears sprang to Heracles's eyes. He felt a sudden stinging pain in his head, and at that moment he believed that was where he'd been struck for he felt no pain elsewhere.

He stared at Linus in bewilderment . . . which turned to loathing. The man's hateful face looked flat and venomous; the skin of his neck was scaly. . . . With a cry of disgust Heracles seized the wooden stool and brought it down with all his gigantic strength on the menacing head before him, crushing it in an instant. The blood ran out of Linus's eyes and mouth in a torrent. . . .

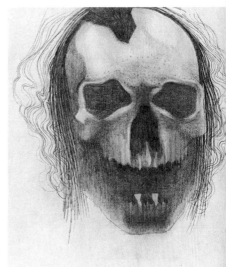

The boy was tried for the crime, but pleaded that he had been struck first. The angry weal raised by the lyre was strong evidence on his behalf; he was acquitted, though there was no doubt that his extreme youth pleaded more eloquently in his favour than the extenuating circumstance. Amphitryon trembled at his immense strength and uncertain nature; and fearing that there might be some fresh outburst of violence from him, sent him to a farm outside of Thebes until such time as the memory of the murder should have faded from the public mind. Whatever hopes Heracles might have nursed of joining the princes on Mount Pelion were now gone forever. The news of such an act as his could not be kept within the walls of Thebes.

The King of Aegina undoubtedly heard of it, and his pride in his own sons must have increased; in particular, the thought of Phorcus, his golden youngest, must have delighted him. Although it was not usual—save in dire calamity or affairs of state— he sent to Mount Pelion for his three sons to return directly. Probably there was no more in his mind than a desire to see them again; but Phorcus was immensely excited: he believed they were being recalled for his father to name him as his heir. He could imagine no other reason; and his brothers, Telamon and Peleus, were inclined to agree. Phorcus's brilliance and fitness to rule were becoming more apparent day by day. Generously they praised him and marvelled at his superiority over themselves. Never were a pair of brothers more proud of their youngest. So the three youths left Mount Pelion with the axe, the stone discus and the silver lyre that the ancient Centaur presented to his departing pupils. Telamon had earned the discus, Peleus the axe, and Phorcus the silver lyre which was the most coveted gift of all, as Chiron valued music as the highest art.

That the three brothers were united in fondness when they reached the isle of Aegina, there can be no doubt. There was even a spirit of youthful playfulness among them; Telamon and Peleus made humorous bows to Phorcus, crowned him with laurel and carried him a-while shoulder-high between them. They ran races on the way—and Phorcus outdistanced them with his usual ease; winning was more than a habit with him, it was an obsession.

Then they came to a field hedged round with low thick trees almost like a tufted wall. Here Telamon proposed a contest with the stone discus; Phorcus agreed, eager to shine yet again, and the three brothers entered the field. Some minutes after, the discus was observed skimming above the trees in a well-thrown curve. Then there was heard a sharp scream—and no more.

Telamon and Peleus emerged from the sheltering trees; their faces were pale, they were breathing heavily. Phorcus was not with them.

Later there was found in the field, clumsily hidden in a patch of long grass, a blood-stained discus and a blood-stained axe. There was no sign of Phorcus or the silver lyre. They were not found till the next day. Phorcus's murdered body was discovered thrust hastily under a bush; the lyre was found later, in another part of the field.

Telamon fled to Salamis, and Peleus to Phthia, from which refuges both brothers vigorously denied the crime; but the only doubt that ever remained was which of the two had felled Phorcus with the discus, and which had then smashed in his head with the axe.

Though the King of Thebes was still father to one murderer, the King of Aegina was now father to two.

Phorcus was buried beside the temple where the king had once given thanks to the gods for his birth. Daily, it seemed, the dead youth's excellence increased until the grand memorial by the temple dwindled to a trifle beside the memorial on his father's lips. Phorcus became such a dream as could live only in a bereaved parent's mind. Long since, the king had plucked out all memory of his other sons. It was the gods who'd taken Phorcus from him—jealous of his skill and beauty.

"Telamon and Peleus were those murdering gods' names," muttered the red-eyed housekeeper to the wandering storyteller who came to Aegina, full of ballads of Titans and gods. "But humour the father if you can."

The storyteller nodded; and in accordance with his art and custom, transfigured the fate of Phorcus into a sunlit tragedy, far removed from the devious deeds of men. The king wept copiously, and rewarded the storyteller with two robes that had once belonged to his now nameless sons.

"You know the gods well, my friend; I envy you the comfort such knowledge must bring."

The storyteller smiled mournfully. As always, it was his fate to create gods for others—and never find them himself. His wanderings had never ceased; and his tale had lengthened with the curiosities he'd picked up. Not long before, he'd been in Aetolia where the Queen of Calydon, in a fit of family pride, had confided that the three Fates themselves had attended the birth of Meleager, her remarkable son. The storyteller had raised his eyebrows; this was something even more distinguished than the usual clutch of goddesses. She'd shown him a half-burnt brand of wood that she treasured, and declared that her son would live for ever, providing the brand was never burned right through. The Fates themselves had said so. . . .

"Yes," murmured the storyteller to the father of murdered Phorcus, "I know the gods as well as anyone does."

He exchanged his threadbare gown for one of the fine pair he'd been given. The years must have shrunk him more than he'd thought—else the King of Aegina's sons must have been of the stature of giants. The robe enveloped him so that he stumbled off like an infant in a shawl—an infant with a face and head as old and brown and wrinkled as a dried olive.

5 • A Gathering of Heroes

Phorcus was dead; his brothers were now with Heracles, living in the shadows. But heroes were plentiful enough; every mother had one, ready and eager to challenge the gods themselves. Here and there, these challenges were taken up; and the wandering storyteller duly recorded the contests, made the defeats more glorious than victory—and walked very carefully lest he trod on an ant, a spider or a lizard that had once been a heroically foolhardy man.

Sometimes, when he'd finished enriching the deeds of some modestly smiling youth who sat reluctantly in the midst of the fireside company, he in his turn would become an audience to the royal father who could always remember hunting boars many times more huge and savage than any that trampled the present woods—and then wonder where such monsters had gone. Then the storyteller would smile, but hold his tongue; there was nothing to be gained by telling these yesterday's warriors that it was not the dangers that had shrunk, but they who'd grown, and that no son could fight the terrors of his father's childhood and defeat them. Every lion would need to be as immense and ghastly as the beast that devastated Nemea, and every snake as venomous and many-headed as the foul Hydra that lurked in the Lernian swamp, to satisfy in full the supernatural fears to which all men were prey.

Then, quite suddenly, there appeared in the woods and fields of Calydon a monster as terrible as it was uncanny and unexplained. It was as if the world had tilted and discharged the huge, violent thing out of some dark cellar to rampage and tear the harvest into tatters and rend the cattle with tusks like great corrupted spears.

It was, or seemed to be, a gigantic boar. Those near enough to see it plainly when it plunged out of the woods described it as being of the size and bulk of a large bull, with abnormally stiff bristles and a snout and immense chest flecked with flowers of foam. On the first night of its appearance, one of the horns of the crescent moon had been seen to be stained with a mist as red as blood; hence it was supposed that the monster had been sent by Artemis, the moon goddess herself, in punishment for a neglect of her altar during the past year.

The King of Calydon himself had been to blame for this, consequently many said it was guilt for having brought the disaster on his people that moved him to proclaim a great hunt to destroy the monster; but equally it might have been merely to indulge his passion for the chase and give his son Meleager an opportunity to confront such a beast as had roamed the world in his father's youth. Or perhaps there was some deeper motive, scarcely understood by the king himself, when he sent his panting heralds far and wide to summon princes to come with spears and arrows and hounds to hunt beside the matchless Meleager and earn such crumbs of glory as they could.

Telamon was the first to arrive, from Salamis where he'd confessed to his brother's murder and been granted forgiveness, at least by men; but when he came face to face with Meleager, he dropped his gaze and looked away. The last time they'd seen each other had been at Chiron's cave when the three brothers had waved a bright farewell to all the company on Mount Pelion. Though Telamon had been purified in the eyes of the law, the stain had not gone when he looked with the more searching eyes of his own heart; hence he was always first to answer any call—such as this hunt in Calydon—where there was danger and the possibility of a heroic end to a shadowed life.

In spite of Meleager's open and friendly greeting and kindly efforts to put him at his ease, there were long and awkward silences between them, and both young men were thankful when the next day brought other hunting princes, many of whom were companions of their days on Mount Pelion, to distract the time from guilty thoughts. Then a second shadow fell upon the company; Peleus joined them, coming from Phthia where he, too, had been purified of his part in his brother's murder. But Peleus, handsome, smiling Peleus, seemed to have left all trouble behind. He came arm in arm with Eurytion, adopted son of

Phthia's king, and already like a brother to Peleus himself. He greeted everyone with honest, fearless eyes, had lively memories of Chiron's cave to exchange with each and all; he never seemed to stop laughing—until he came to Telamon. Then his eyes clouded, his lips tightened and a look passed between the brothers as cold and stern as death.

The princes were quartered together in a stone and timber hunting-lodge, built on rising ground overlooking the wood where the monster had its lair. Though none had seen the creature, its wild bellowings were heard by night, silencing for a time the pleasant uproar of the young men eager for the hunt.

For nine days Meleager's great father feasted them and regaled them with tales as long as the nights, of boars, bulls and wild stallions he'd hunted before his guests were born. His deep-set eyes, bright with firelight, would range from prince to prince— from smiling Peleus to grave Jason of Iolcus, to Admetus who always looked older than he was, and Theseus of Athens whose broad brow shone as if with an inner light, and shadowy Telamon . . . and then he would glance, with massive pride, to the leader of the hunt, Meleager, his son. The intent faces, bending forward on smooth, youthful necks, seemed like a strange, flickering vision of dream-heroes; it was as if the father was seeing the bright company through the eyes of the little withered storyteller who'd crept through Calydon some long while ago. . . . Then would come the dreadful sound of bellowing and tearing of branches from the shaking night outside, and he wondered if perhaps the dangers were greater now, and the monsters more terrible than in the days of his youth.

On the morning of the tenth day the princes gathered in the courtyard of the lodge. There was a stout breeze blowing so that the sky was fitfully overcast with cloud; and in the changing light the burnished spears, javelins and quivers tufted with white arrow feathers seemed to shiver like a bronze forest full of marvellous snared birds. Here and there, lean hounds, not yet on the leash, padded about, pausing to nuzzle some huntsman bending to tighten his sandal cords—or to cock an impudent leg against a convenient spear.

Meleager was everywhere, instructing the company in the discipline of the hunt; no purpose would be served, he said, by needlessly rushing into danger. He urged this particularly on

Telamon, who, he sensed, was most likely to seek a separate heroism. It was indeed to Telamon he was speaking when there was a commotion near the gate. A late arrival, but come just in time for the beginning of the hunt.

Meleager turned as the newcomer, as was proper, approached him; he caught his breath. . . .

Grey eyes stared into his; lips curved in a smile half hostile, half defensive; but there was nothing defensive about the newcomer's strung bow and quiver of arrows flighted by a very skilful hand.

Forgetful of Telamon and, indeed, of everyone else at that moment, Meleager felt the blood rush to his cheeks under the young woman's gaze; for it was a girl who stood before him, though at first glance he'd taken her for a boy. She was tall, with long fair hair caught up in a loose knot at the back of her neck. . . .

"My name is Atalanta," she said, smiling at Meleager's confusion. "My father is King of Argos, and I have come to join you in the hunt."

There was a brief silence, then came a murmur of protest from among the princes who had gathered round. Hunting was not for women. . . .

"Artemis is a woman," said Meleager, sharply, feeling his leadership was in question; "and she is the goddess of the hunt."

"I would not care to hunt beside Artemis," said Eurytion amusedly. "She is also the goddess of sudden death." Peleus, standing beside him, laughed as if to turn everything to good humour, when Meleager's two uncles put in their oar and advised their nephew somewhat pompously against allowing Atalanta's presence.

Meleager shared his father's dislike of these two men, in particular of Plexippus who was all too generous with advice and inclined to give himself airs of ruling the kingdom through his doting sister, the queen. Perhaps, had these two men kept out of it, Meleager might have been persuaded by his friends, but now he was awkwardly placed. Atalanta, observing the keen situation, smiled at Meleager with scarcely concealed mockery. But she spoke courteously.

"I came to you as I heard that you were the leader of the hunt, Prince Meleager."

"And so I am," he said abruptly. Then, raising his voice, he cried out: "Those of you who are afraid to match your courage

against a woman's had better stay behind. If need be, she and I will hunt the boar alone!"

No one could reject such a challenge; there was a great rattling of arrows in quivers—as of a sudden flight of starlings—and the huntsmen moved to their fixed places beyond the courtyard gates. Here, on the edge of a broad, grassy slope which dipped down to the wood, Meleager had drawn up the hunt in a deep half-moon with the swiftest princes on the flanks. There was a moment of stillness while the gods' blessing was asked for the enterprise; spears dipped, and the hounds, now leashed in, strained forward against outstretched arms; only the wind still raced and ruffled the hair of the crescent of princes so that it seemed that the motionless hunt and the tilting disc of green itself had taken to the air in a gravely flying enchantment.

Then Meleager's mother, the lovely Queen of Calydon, came to embrace her brothers and smilingly wish her son success. She had no fears for his safety; she remembered—as if it was yesterday—the misty hour following her baby's birth when she lay watching the firelight dancing on the ceiling. Three huge blind women had fumbled their way into the chamber, filling the air with a strong goatish smell; even in her exhausted state, she had recognized the Fates.

"Meleager will live so long as the brand in the fire remains unconsumed," they had muttered, fingering the edge of the crib. Then they had vanished as mysteriously as they had come; and she had crawled from her bed to put out the fire with water from the bowls in which tiny Meleager had been washed. She had dragged the soaked brand back to her bed and would not be parted from it, even though everyone declared she had had no more than a delirious dream. Since that time she had guarded the brand as jealously as life itself. Her husband and brothers had often smiled at her fantastic notion; even the wrinkled little storyteller to whom she had shown it—in an access of supernatural pride—had looked doubtful, though polite. Nonetheless she had held to her beliefs; and now, even though her son went out to hunt a monster sent by the moon goddess herself, she felt no alarm for him. Thanks to her care of the half-burnt brand, Meleager would live for ever; the Fates had promised, and not even the cruel gods could alter the decrees of the Fates. . . .

Meleager's mother smiled proudly as the curve of princes moved down the slope towards the quiet wood.

6 • The Boar Hunt

The forest was full of little fawn ghosts shivering in and out of the darkness as though seeking to unravel it; sniffing the ground, sniffing the air, flickering rapidly along the reeded water-courses where crippled willows dragged at their roots. The hounds were free and running; the whole forest reeked with the sour, dangerous smell of boar.

Then came the princes, moving through the patched shadows like the armed spirits of the trees: Theseus of Athens, smooth as marble, so that blood trickling from briar scratches on his thighs seemed astonishing and unnatural; golden Jason, wraithlike in his passing . . . then Prince Admetus, Peleus, Telamon, immortal Meleager himself—all watchful, intent; massive hands gripping javelins . . . And on the right of the princes, deftly threading the trees, moved the strange, fierce young woman who claimed to be the King of Argos's daughter.

From time to time Meleager glimpsed her, crossing a clearing so swiftly and silently that she seemed like an image that the mind prints on air, then dissolves into leaves, branches and shadows. Great agitation filled him; she was as lovely as Artemis herself. Indeed, there were moments when Meleager wondered if she was the goddess, come to hunt down her own monstrous boar. He began to fear for himself and his ever-increasing longing for the girl. Artemis was the virgin goddess, and there was neither hope nor help for the man who desired her.

Artemis's spirit was very strong in the forest; there was no mistaking the supernatural quietness in the air; even the sound of the wind was muffled and the only evidence of it was the fitful effect of clouds being tumbled across the invisible sky: sudden darknesses swept through the trees like the shadows of huge wings. Meleager shivered as he recalled Eurytion's words: "Artemis is also the goddess of sudden death." In which guise was she watching the forest: huntress, virgin—or death?

Again he saw Atalanta, now with an arrow notched in her bow. He longed to cross the line of the hunt and be beside her; but he saw Plexippus, his interfering uncle, watching him for just such a wayward act, so he kept to his place, though with beating heart and furious eyes.

Presently the ground began to dip towards a deep hollow formed by the meeting of three water-courses. Vague swampy glimmerings could be seen among the thick reeds and marsh-grass, then there was darkness. . . . Here and there, on the edge of the hollow, were strewn branches newly wrenched from nearby trunks, and in one place a young oak lay snapped through the trunk as if it had been no more than a twig.

The hounds began to utter short, whimpering cries such as beasts commonly give when an unnatural presence, sensed only by them, is near at hand.

The hunting princes moved on, but slowly now; arrows clicked and rustled from quivers, bows creaked as great arms bent them, and the bronze tips of levelled javelins glinted menacingly as they swung towards the wall of darkness beyond the reeds.

Ancaeus, the great Arcadian, who was posted on the extreme left, fingered the edge of his two-headed axe and cursed his ill-luck in being so far removed from the chance of drawing first blood. He had advanced perhaps two paces when the air was dimmed by one of the sudden blacknesses that had plagued the hunt since it began. He paused, shivering; then the boar broke cover. He had just sufficient time to raise his axe, but no time to bring it down before he was changed—in a bellowing instant—from an eager golden hero to a mangled heap of blood and bowels. Though he'd turned his head, he could have glimpsed no more than something dark and gigantic rushing down upon him before he was ripped to pieces and tossed aside. The monster had come, not from the wall of darkness, but from behind him on the treacherous left.

The goddess was in the forest—as virgin, huntress, and sudden death. With smeared tusks and blazing eyes the moon boar raged across the hollow, swerving murderously to uproot bushes, young trees and screaming hounds that spattered the leaves with sudden blood.

The hunting princes were seized with dread; so great was the speed of the creature that each saw it rushing at him in his own private terror; madness spread like a plague; shadows, trees seemed to be the beast. The air was filled with spears, arrows, javelins—quivering into tree-trunks, vanishing like glinting lightnings into the recesses of leaves. A young man lay shrieking against a scarred maple tree, blood gushing from the backs of his knees where the sinews had been ripped like loose threads; forever now a cripple to tell over and over again the tale of his last adventure when with Theseus, Jason, Admetus and great Meleager himself he hunted the Calydonian boar.

Telamon, mad for glory, rushed forward, caught his foot against a willow root, and fell. Peleus dragged him back—and the ground shook as the monster went raging by like a thunderbolt. It saw Atalanta, kneeling in its path as cold and lovely as its divine mistress. Her eyes were shining, her bow was stretched. The boar bellowed and swerved. Atalanta smiled. . . .

"Blood! First blood!" shouted Meleager.

A bristle with a feathered tip seemed suddenly to have sprouted from behind the boar's left ear. It was Atalanta's arrow.

The creature faltered, shook its huge head in a fine crimson rain, and tore at the ground with its hooves for another charge. But its course was run. Meleager sprang forward and plunged his javelin into the mountainous back. The boar screamed; steam and stained froth issued from its snout; then it grunted and fell on its side. The monster of the moon goddess was dead.

But this was not the only death in the forest. Pinned to the trunk of an oak tree by a javelin through his neck, hung Eurytion, prince of Phthia; and the weapon was that of fatal Peleus. Whether by chance or the design of the gods, Peleus was a murderer a second time, and for a second time an outcast of mankind.

High up to the left of the hollow some three or four hounds nosed among the remains of Ancaeus, one-time prince of Arcadia, and wonderfully deft with the two-headed axe. Such was the sport of Artemis, goddess of the hunt; nor was she finished with the princes yet.

Exultantly Meleager set his foot on the neck of the dead boar.

"To Atalanta!" he proclaimed. "Hers was first blood; hers are the tusks and pelt. The monster was already dying from her arrow when I struck!"

Atalanta came forward to claim her arrow from its fatal resting place, when Plexippus contemptuously pushed the girl aside. He stood with legs apart and hands on hips, scowling at the leader of the hunt.

"You arrogant love-sick boy," he said angrily. "Do you fancy these princes and I will stand by and let you give the glory of the hunt to a woman? Do you think we are here only to pander to your desires? Take the spoils for yourself—or give them to whoever stands next to you in eminence. Do it now, nephew!"

Meleager, biting his lip, affected not to hear. "Atalanta!" he cried, holding out his hand to the huntress; but Plexippus, incensed at being ignored, furiously knocked his hand aside.

"Insolent boy . . ." he began, when Meleager, feeling Atalanta's mocking eyes upon him, could endure no more. He turned on Plexippus with the accumulated venom of many years.

"Insolent old man!" he shouted. His sword was in his hand. Plexippus glared at it—as if divining the outcome before Meleager himself. He tried to utter a warning—but the very look of reproof on his face brought on the calamity.

"Murderer—murderer!" screamed Plexippus's brother, amazed to see Plexippus spouting blood from his pierced belly; then Meleager turned on him, too, and buried the sword, red from one uncle's blood, deep in the chest of the other. He was drunk with death—and another cup of it mattered little. The strange violence in the forest rendered all things trifling.

Thus far the terrible goddess had exacted four deaths for her boar. Her hunting had been the more successful. But her presence lingered and would not depart. There was Meleager himself, the god-child of the Fates.

Pale as death, the Queen of Calydon saw messengers, with dipped spears and bowed heads, come out of the forest and mount the slope. Not Meleager dead? Her beloved son! Why was he not first to come? He could not die! The Fates had promised—and she'd kept the brand for all these years. Wherever she went, even to the far corners of the kingdom, she had taken it with her—shutting her ears and eyes to gentle mockery and pitying smiles for a mother's foolish care. She had believed in the Fates; all the security of her life had been anchored to their promise.

The messengers' faces were grief-stricken and uneasy, as if

they dreaded to tell their news.

Meleager—Meleager! The queen fled to the room in the lodge that had been set aside for her. She opened the oak chest that always accompanied her; she fell on her knees and thanked the gods. The brand was still there. Clutching it to her breast she ran back across the courtyard to the gates.

The messengers had reached the king. She saw him listening gravely. He turned to glance towards the lodge. Even from the distance she saw his face was grim and shadowed—as if the news he'd heard would be heaviest for her to bear.

Once more dread seized the queen, and all the nagging doubts of the years sprang out on her. What if her dream had been only a dream and the precious brand no more than a piece of half-burnt wood, preserved out of a delirium?

She felt the heat of a fire that had been kindled to burn the entrails of the beast if it should be killed. She backed away, fearful of a stray spark igniting the brand. With all her heart and soul she still clung to the Fates' prophecy till the Fates themselves should prove it false.

The messengers had left the king; they were approaching her. She held her head high, as became the Queen of Calydon.

"The great boar has been killed, lady."

"The gods be praised. Whose was the glory?"

"Your son, great queen; matchless Meleager. His was the javelin . . ."

"I thank the gods again. Is he—unharmed?"

The messengers hesitated, and then nodded. Tears of gladness started in the queen's eyes. What else mattered so long as her son was unharmed?

"Then why the dipped spears? Why the dull looks?"

"Not for your son, lady."

The queen frowned; then she saw, coming from the forest, first the fierce, beautiful Atalanta, and then, stepping a little behind her, Meleager. He went towards the king, his father. She saw his sword was streaked with blood.

"Then who—?"

The messengers looked away.

"Your brothers, great queen. Your brothers are dead."

Her son was with his father now; the princess of Argos was by his side. The king was nodding. . . . Dully the queen tried to understand what had befallen her; a loneliness pierced her heart. Her dearest brothers . . . the living dreams of her life before Calydon . . . the sharers in the forbidden secrets of a child's happiness—all gone.

"The—the boar? They fell to—to its tusks, then?"

The messengers began to back away. "They are dead, madam."

"*Was* it the monster?"

"It was your son. Meleager killed them."

Her son, her husband and the woman from Argos were still together; they were watching the forest. The dead were being brought out; and the monstrous boar, like a huge black blot, was being dragged by a dozen men towards the easy prince.

Then the queen's heart cracked. She screamed aloud in wild despair; and flung the long-treasured brand into the fire. There was nothing left for her to believe in, neither the gods nor the Fates. All her life she had been deceived by that ancient dream. The accursed brand had never been more than a foolish talisman of her mother's love and longing to protect. Now her murderous son had betrayed her. . . .

Suddenly Meleager turned from his father and the huntress by his side. He looked towards his mother standing in the gates. He waved to her—she caught the glint of a smile—then a shadow crossed his beloved face. She saw his brows contract, his features begin to pucker as they'd often done when, as a sleeping child, some disturbing dream had crossed his innocent mind. She'd always comforted him then. . . .

"Meleager!" she sobbed. "My son—" The fire beside her leaped and roared. The brand was veiled in tall flames that took on the aspect of three blind stumbling figures, with clawing arms.

"*Meleager!*" She fell on her knees and plunged her hands into the fire. It blazed and collapsed, blistering and charring her skin. Branch after flaring branch she dragged out; but the brand she sought fell further and further into the heart of the fire. At last her hands, now melting in the agonising heat, reached it. She grasped it; it crumbled away into nothingness. Long keeping had rendered it dry and eager for the burning.

She crawled away, her hands and ashes all one. She stared towards her son. He was staggering, clutching at his chest.

"I am burning—I am burning!" she heard him cry. The king hastened to support him; but the prince had already fallen. The Fates had kept their promise; Meleager was dead.

The hunt of the Calydonian boar was finished; the burned queen stared blindly down at the ruins of it as if she and the silent figures were already no more than a dreadful ancient dream in which nothing was real but the gods and the implacable Fates.

7 • A Second Life

With heavy steps and darkened faces the princes left the house of mourning and returned to their kingdoms; while to those palaces where none would be coming back, messengers with dipped spears travelled to tell of the tragedies in Calydon, softening the blow as best they could and honouring the dead.

Each prince recounted the hunt in his own manner, for to each it had been a strangely private day. But for Peleus there were no listeners by the fire, no housekeeper to spread his deeds among the servants; he dared not return to Phthia and confess to the death of Eurytion. Instead, he went with Jason to Iolcus; Jason took pity on this unlucky man . . . though it was a pity that was keenly watchful.

He saw Peleus's greatness and many excellences; he also saw the fatal flaw that, in spite of them, rendered him a treacherous vessel. He divined Peleus's hapless dread of being surpassed; for it was a dread more than an envy that sprang out upon him suddenly. He expected it no more than those who incurred it; his handsome smiles and open-hearted laughter were no mask concealing a corrupt and devious soul, they were as much a part of him as was the jealousy that fatally blinded him. So wise Jason walked very carefully beside the man he'd chosen to shelter.

But of all the heroes who returned from Calydon, there was one who went with a sense of peace and satisfaction: Admetus of Pherae, the richest and most fortunate of all. Not only a lovely wife awaited him, but a father and mother as proud and loving as luckless Meleager's had proved otherwise. Had there been a brand to secure Admetus's life, not even the hands of a god could have wrested it from his parents' safe keeping. Such was the love of this aged couple that they'd given up the throne itself to their splendid son and to Alcestis, his wife. They were content to be his pensioners and live out their days in the reflection of his glory. Greater love than theirs Admetus had yet to see. Nonetheless he could not help reflecting that his own more regular life had gone some way towards earning this love. Not for him the unnatural charms of Atalanta. . . .

Small wonder that Admetus returned to Pherae well pleased with himself. When he considered the death of Meleager, his thoughts were not, "There but for the grace of the gods go I," but, "Here, by my own respectable manner of living, stay I." Even death was not to claim him at first call; no less a god than Apollo had promised him a second lease of life if, when his time came, another from his household would go willingly in his place. Though he was young and in good health, this thought often fascinated him; sometimes, at dead of night, when a stray twinge or passing chill alarmed him, he'd fall to thinking of this aged nurse or that decrepit servant (now wracked with years and rheumatism), who'd doted on him since infancy, and how he'd ask them to part with the last miserable remnants of their days for their beloved Admetus. Then, much comforted, he'd smile and settle back to sleep. . . .

His homecoming was as glowing as he'd expected; love, love everywhere. Smiling faces greeted him, bright eyes were fixed on him, and eager voices clamoured to hear the tale of his adventures over and over again. A lesser man would have grown weary of it; but Admetus thrived and expanded. Love and admiration were meat and wine to him; not that he neglected the feast that had been prepared. When he'd bathed and put on fresh robes, he showed the company that a hero's stomach was no less great than his heart. He ate and drank with a marvellous fury—as if he was defeating the great boar of Calydon all over again, but this time with his jaws. For it must be admitted that, in the excitement of his tellings, he had been trapped into enlarging his own part in the hunt.

At last he staggered from the table, supported by laughing Alcestis.

"And now for another hunt!" he shouted, fumbling his blushing queen's waist with his great straying hand. "And another battle. The battle of love!"

"Tomorrow, my lord," laughed Alcestis. "Tonight you should sleep away your journey—and your feast!"

But Admetus was too full of ardour and triumph to be denied. Quenching the protests of Alcestis with fond but haphazard kisses, he reeled away to his bedchamber, vowing that he and Alcestis would beget such a hero that night as would outshine a cityful of your Meleagers and Jasons and murdering Peleuses. The door slammed, the bronze bolt slid to, and sounds of kisses and laughter and amorous cries were heard for a truly heroic time. At last they died away into a deep and snoring silence.

"Admetus . . . royal Admetus."

He woke up. Someone had called his name, but so softly that Alcestis, lying in a shipwreck of linen and a storm of hair, never stirred.

"Admetus, my friend. . . ."

He struggled to sit up; but there seemed to be a heavy weight on his chest that drove sharp edges into him as he strained.

"King of Pherae. . . ."

There was something by the door; a tall, uncertain thread of silver that wove and glinted in the dark air. Here and there it blurred and smudged into the edge of a roundness, as if someone had begun to draw an arm, a shoulder, the outline of a face. . . .

"Do you not know me, Admetus?"

The rippling, running thread of silver sketched a curious, sideways smile.

"I am Hermes, my friend, messenger of death. Alas! your hour has struck and I am come to take you from this world. Admetus, you must die."

Not comprehending what had befallen him, Admetus glared at the dreadful apparition by the door.

"My friend, my office pleases me no more than it pleases you. I promise you, I don't come by my own choice, but we must all obey the Fates. Come, Admetus . . . ."

Then Admetus understood. "No, no!" he whispered, when he remembered the promise of a second life. He clasped his hands before him and with tears streaming down his face, reminded the Messenger that he alone of all mankind was to be given a second chance.

"Ah," sighed Hermes. "If only Meleager had had such influence. But who can rival Admetus for love? Go, my friend, and find someone who will willingly take your place at my side. You have a day. . . ."

"An hour will be enough!" cried Admetus; for this was an occasion he'd long planned for in his dreams.

"Take a day," advised Hermes. "You may need longer than you suppose, Admetus, King of Pherae."

His nurse—his ancient, wrinkled nurse who always smelled of washed linen and mint! He stumbled down the corridors to the little room where as a child he used to creep for comfort from bad dreams. Now the dream was hideous, and the comfort most necessary. He woke the old woman urgently.

"My lord Admetus—you are a grown man now. There are others more proper to soothe you. The lady Alcestis. . . ."

"Hermes has come for me! I must die!"

She sat up, her thin hair peeling round her head like dead grass. Her eyes unwrinkled in terror.

"Alas—my darling Admetus! So soon? Oh, the gods are cruel, cruel!" She began to weep and her bony shoulders rattled with noisy grief.

"But there is still hope," cried Admetus eagerly. "If you will take my place I may yet be saved!"

The old woman's eyes wrinkled up again. She peered at Admetus somewhat craftily.

"I would be honoured, my lord. When must I go?"

"Now! Directly!"

"Alas, Admetus! If only it had been next year. I must see my daughter and her children in the country next month. I promised them. Oh, my lord, if only it had been next year!"

"Heartless old crone!" shouted Admetus. "By next year you'll be dead anyway! Where is the love you had for me?"

He stumbled from the room with her cries and lamentations pursuing him. "Alas for Admetus! So young, so fine—the flower of the land! Weep for Admetus who dies so young!"

Her quavering voice dwindled away in the twists and turns of the palace as Admetus rushed from room to room, engaged on the most desperate search in the world. At last he found the man he sought; a one-time gardener, now bent like a hoop with age so that even in sleep he lay as if toiling with a spade. Many a time this old man had shown the little prince bright flowers and rare herbs—and sworn that Admetus was the rarest plant that ever grew; for which, times without number, he'd been kissed on both his weathered cheeks by the affectionate child.

Gently Admetus shook him awake. "Old man—dear, good old man! Hermes has come for your Admetus. I must die!"

The ancient fellow blinked piteously up at the king.

"Unless—unless *you* will take my place!"

"Eh?"

"Die for me."

The old man shook his head and with his crippled fingers reamed out his thick ears.

"Will you die for me?" shrieked Admetus.

"I'm deaf, my lord. If I knew what you wanted I'd oblige directly. But I'm deaf, you see."

"Then I'll write it down—"

The old man's filmy eyes glittered abruptly. "Can't read," he said, overcoming one disadvantage only to fall victim to another; then he resumed his air of dull amazement and willingness to help if only he knew how.

"Old devil!" raged the king. "Where is the love you had for me?"

Already the night was fading and the beginnings of morning were creeping into the palace, uncovering columns, marble halls and gorgeous tapestries; but they were as lonely as the grave: all living souls seemed to have vanished as blossoms before the wind. Despairingly Admetus dragged himself from pillar to pillar, his lamed heart beating painfully.

"Alas for Admetus! Cut off in the flower of his life. Shed your tears for Admetus!"

The endless wailing of the broken-hearted nurse echoed through the deserted halls. A feeble rage seized the king as he thought of the wretched old woman clinging so selfishly to her last few miserable weeks; then his anger passed into a dreadful dullness and he began to make his way to a part of the palace that hitherto he had avoided.

Suddenly he paused. He had seen a child hopping across a

patch of floor that had been inlaid with a design to catch the first
rays of the morning sun. Fascinated, Admetus watched, and
wondered what part of the pattern the child was avoiding. He
remembered, when he was a child he'd hopped between the
figures, for it had been bad luck to land on them. Sensing the
scrutiny, the child looked up and, seeing the intent king, smiled
with innocent pride.

He would die for me! thought Admetus with a thrill of hope.
He's so young—what can he know about it? He'll say yes to
flatter me. He'll not understand what's being asked of him. . . .

Nonetheless, Admetus hesitated—when a serving-woman ran
out from behind a pillar to snatch the child away. He saw from
her pleading and terror-stricken face that she had read his mind.

I could ask her! he thought suddenly. Surely she'd do anything to spare her child! *She* would die for me. And yet . . . it
would not be willingly. . . .

"Go!" said Admetus harshly, and dragged himself on towards
that sad and shameful hope he had always thrust to the back of
his mind.

But when all was said and done, he reflected, they were quite
desperately ancient and had lived long beyond all expectation.
Many times they must think mournfully on their younger days.
The sight of each other's wrinkles must be very depressing. The
sadness would be more his than theirs; he would not be asking so
very much. . . .

They were sitting side by side when he entered their room,
enjoying the morning through their opened casement.

"My son," murmured his father, rising to greet him. "We
have heard."

There was silence as he looked at them—a heavy silence; then
the nurse's lamentations quivered on the air: "Weep for Admetus—weep for him!"

"Father," whispered the doomed son; but further words
stuck in his throat. They must have known why he'd come; why
were they *forcing* the cruel words from him?

"He has come to bid us farewell," muttered his mother
abruptly. She continued to stare out of the casement, but her
twisted fingers gripped the arm of her chair.

"My son," mumbled Admetus's father brokenly, "were it for
me alone, I would gladly die for you; but I have your mother to

think of. She—she would not let me—"

"He has come only to bid us farewell," repeated his mother, not moving. "We have given him life once; he cannot ask it of us again."

"Your mother, my son . . . I cannot leave her—"

"We have given him the kingdom; what more can he ask of us? He has come only to take his last leave."

Frozenly the son listened. . . .

"Weep for Admetus; shed your tears for Admetus . . ." came the nurse's mournful wail.

"You are a famous hero, Admetus," said his father, with a semblance of sternness that ill became him. "And like a hero you go uncomplaining when you are summoned."

"We will not be the first parents to lose a glorious child," said his mother, as immovable as ever.

"They say those whom the gods love best, die young. Olympus must love you dearly, my son."

"I would sooner be loved by Pherae," sighed Admetus bitterly.

"When he was a child I would have died for him; there would have been a need. But now he is grown; he has his own world . . . the love is different; it returns to the husband as it was before he began."

"Your mother speaks the truth, Admetus. Though we still love you dearly, we love each other too."

"He thinks because we are old, we shrink from the sight of each other; he thinks we no longer love the warmth of the sun, the smell of flowers, the sound of birds singing. He thinks we are all but dead already."

Admetus saw the withered hand twist and tighten. He saw it was shining in the morning light; it was running over with tears that were falling ceaselessly from her hidden face.

"Farewell, Admetus, my glorious son . . . ."

The marble floor struck cold against his naked feet; he shuddered; soon a deeper chill would be invading him. He made his way back to his bedchamber to await the second coming of Hermes, messenger of the dead. He entered quietly so as not to awaken Alcestis; the thought of bidding her farewell was more than he could endure.

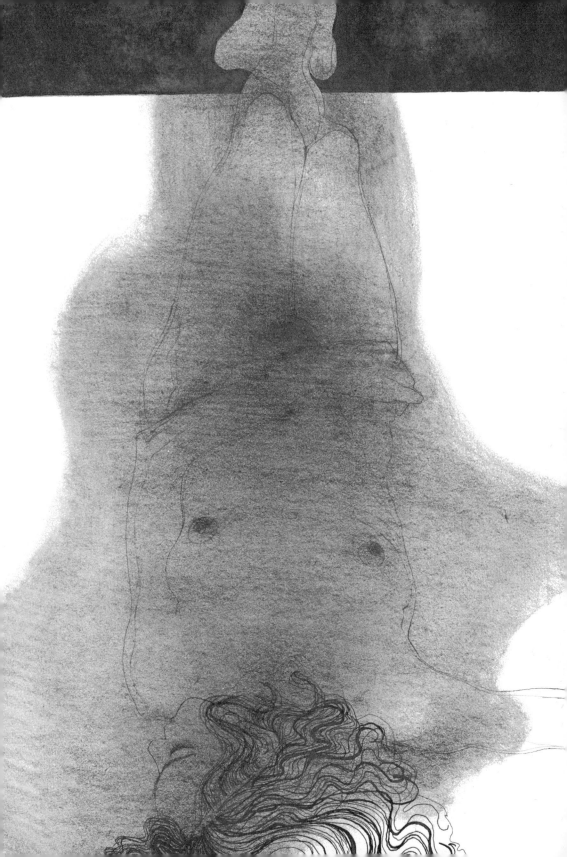

"Admetus, my lord?"

He had delayed too long; she was already awake. She lay on her side watching for him; her face was pale and her eyes heavy with broken sleep. He did not know what to say; he wished with all his heart that he'd been dead a thousand years when all his griefs and conflicts would have been smoothed to the unfeeling contours of a legend.

"Come to me, Admetus. I want you to embrace me once more. For the last time, my lord."

She knew. Admetus straightened his shoulders and lifted up his head. He crossed the room with a firm step; nothing was to be gained by adding to his wife's distress.

He knelt to take Alcestis in his arms—when something clattered and fell. He looked down and saw that he had knocked over a cup that had been standing beside the bed. Some drops of liquid trickled out and soaked into the dappled goatskin that covered the marble floor. He set the cup upright and at once an ancient, musty smell arose . . . a smell of darkness and mice. Admetus frowned—he grew pale—he cried out. The cup, the bedside and Alcestis's parted lips reeked of death. She had drunk hemlock.

"Why—?" he began in unthinking anguish, when she raised her hand and pressed her fingers against his lips. She shook her head.

"My poor Admetus . . . so bewildered, so hurt with the world. Looking . . . asking . . . begging . . . but there was no one. . . . Alas, you asked too much, my dear . . . men must ever love life more than each other. It would be a sad world, husband, if when the light went out for one, all were plunged into darkness. . . ."

Her eyelids fluttered; she sighed, filling the air with the fatal scent of hemlock. She went on, but her voice was diminished to a whisper . . . and her thoughts seemed to wander, as if her mind had already lost its hold on them.

"They say old Prometheus knows a great secret concerning Zeus that could free him from his rock of pain; but he holds his tongue and endures, just to show us, his well-loved little creatures, that even agony such as his can be borne . . . and that the sight of the world makes all worthwhile."

Alcestis's finger fell away from her husband's lips. He reached to hold her hand; it was cold. For a moment he thought she was already dead. But she smiled:

"Why, my dear, didn't you come to me first of all? Didn't you think that I would die for you, Admetus? Had you so—so little faith in my love?"

"Alcestis! I loved you too much to ask! Alcestis, my wife—I never thought, never dreamed, never wanted life without you!"

"You will, my love . . . we all do . . . remember Prometheus . . . remember Alcestis—ah!"

Something dark and enormous seemed to sweep into the room. Admetus flung his arms round his wife; but he was brushed aside by shadows that seemed to suffocate him like a mountain of ash and cobwebs. Dimly, through veils and veils of tears, he saw Alcestis lifted from her poisoned shell of flesh and wrapped in arms of black. Then she was gone. Hades himself had taken her; Admetus was left to endure his promised second life.

8 • The Miracle at Pherae

Tall, dark-haired and with clear grey eyes that continually hovered between thoughts and dreams, a young man stood at the palace gates. He carried neither sword nor dagger nor two-headed axe; instead he leaned on a thick staff, or club, rather, of wild olive wood. His strong legs were travel-stained from sandal to knee.

"My name," he said to the gate-keeper, "is Heracles of Thebes."

The gate-keeper hesitated, looked doubtful. Certainly the young man did not appear as powerful and commanding as he'd always imagined the famous captain of the Theban armies; yet he couldn't help remembering the oft-told tale of the strangled serpents and the terrible rage that had finished off the unlucky Linus. Uneasily he stood aside.

The young man restrained a smile at the gate-keeper's discomfort, and entered the courtyard. The gate-keeper made as if to go after him—to explain—to warn him that the time was unsuitable; but Heracles was already mounting the steps that led to the portico.

He was surprised at the quietness everywhere; he had always heard that the palace at Pherae was lively and hospitable . . . else he would never have come.

"My name," he said courteously to a withered old nurse or serving-woman who shuffled between the high pillars, "is Heracles of Thebes."

He smiled gently as he spoke. It always pleased him to see the aged well cared for and kept in comfort when their years of service were long since done; it showed a generous heart and a master who was worthy of his place.

"Will you take me to King Admetus?"

At once a frightened, guilty look crossed the old woman's face;

she began to shake her head and back away, when she was interrupted.

"I am Admetus."

The old woman started. "It is Heracles, my lord . . . Heracles of Thebes has come . . . only—only he does not know—"

Admetus, who had never looked young, now seemed aged by more than years. His eyes were sunken, his lips were cracked and bitten.

"You did well," he said to the old woman who was now shuffling away in ancient alarm; "we do not impose our own private griefs on others. It would be a sad world," he added, his deep eyes suddenly glistening, "if when the light went out for one, all were plunged into darkness."

Heracles bowed his head and wished deeply he had not come to this house of guilty sadness. It made him ashamed of his own light-heartedness. He longed to ask what grief had fallen on Pherae, but he respected Admetus's reticence.

Admetus offered him his hand and began to lead him to the great hall, asking him of his own affairs and what had brought him to Pherae. Heracles smiled; he had been to Oechalia to choose a wife and dowry for one of his sons. Young as he was, he was already the proud father of four sons and he was honourably engaged in finding them kingdoms and crowns. He smiled even more broadly as he thought of tipsy golden chaplets clapped on his children's heads, quite extinguishing with grandeur all but their mischievous eyes.

Then his private thoughts gave way to unease and curiosity once more as he walked beside Admetus. Courtiers and servants seemed to avoid them; an old, old man, bent like a hoop, hobbled wretchedly away, casting dreary, fearful glances at the king as if he expected vengeance to fall on him for some unknown crime.

They came to the great hall; beams of sunlight struck through the high casements, dividing the air into a dusty golden cage.

"The lady Alcestis!" exclaimed Heracles. "Is it she, beside the pillar?"

He pointed—and Admetus stared in anguish. He saw nothing but shadows. Servants in the room looked to one another in horror . . . Heracles frowned.

"What is wrong, Admetus? Why do you tremble when I point

out your wife? Why do the servants creep away? And why does Alcestis stare and stare from the shadows? Look, my friend—look at her—"

"She is dead, Heracles. She died not long before you came. She drank hemlock and died so that I might live. It was a bargain with the gods. I—I asked others . . . others who might have died for me . . . I thought—but none, none would . . . and I came back and Alcestis, Heracles . . . I did not ask . . . I—I—"

Admetus fell silent, and Heracles divined the immensity of his shame and grief. His young heart ached for this quiet, generous man whose only crime seemed to have been a love of life. His eyes filled with tears; he looked away from Admetus—and saw once more the frail ghost of lovely Alcestis. The shadows seemed to be sucking her away like a great dark tide. She drifted, drifted between the pillars. . . . An outstretched arm was drawn back and folded into the blackness. Her mouth opened to call, and was blotted out . . . and her eyes were swiftly bandaged with cobwebs. . . . She seemed to be floating in a sea of dust. . . .

"It is the will of the gods, Heracles," muttered Admetus.

The haunted dust seemed to flow like a torrent out of all the apertures in the hall.

"No!" cried Heracles, suddenly consumed with the bright anger of youth. "It is not so, Admetus!"

"Who are we, Heracles, to fight against death?"

Heracles glanced at him in amazement and youthful contempt. "Who is death, Admetus, to fight against us? Better to die in childhood than stretch out our necks as grown men! Is it for this that old Prometheus suffers?"

"Where are you going, Heracles? Where are you rushing in so violent a hurry?"

But Heracles had already passed through the thick sunbeams and was gone from the hall; his voice alone came echoing back to Admetus, but it was indistinct and the words could only be guessed at. Admetus fancied that the young man—so arrogant in his youth and strength—had answered: "To bring her back, Admetus. . . ."

The stricken king shook his head. He was half envious, half angry; the youth had no right . . . and no hope beyond his own wild vanity.

There was a column of darkness on the road from Pherae to Aornum; a tall, writhing column that travelled at an immense speed. Its shape changed continually; at times it seemed scarcely taller than a man, then it swelled and seemed to touch the sky with tattered claws. Yet it produced no movement in the air; no wind of passing. The tufts of roadside grass, the stunted bushes and even the crushed pebbles directly in its path remained quiet and unmoved. Sometimes the blackness seemed streaked with greyish white—as if it was bearing something away in its gloomy depths; then these flecks vanished and all was racing darkness once more.

The only thing that neither changed nor faltered was its relentless speed; and the young man who sped in its wake for mile after mile groaned with the effort of keeping it in sight. His sandals had long since broken away and his naked feet printed his passage with blood from a dozen or more cuts and scratches from the rough ground.

Fiercely Heracles increased his pace; the dark column grew larger and detail in it became more distinct. Its weird, cobwebby texture seemed composed of many heads and faces, with black eye-sockets and toothless holes for mouths . . . like a gown of silent screams. Then a woman's hair streamed out, rich and lovely—only to be roughly bandaged back into the suffocating dark.

Hatred, disgust, anger and pity filled him. He could run faster yet; the world flew by him as he and the brutish god of death ate up the merciless road to Aeornum, where there was an entrance into hell.

Not far to the west of Pherae is a crossroads. Along the lesser of the two roads hobbled a singularly shrunken figure. Burned a dirty brown by the sun, wrinkled by years and wind, and clutching at his outsize, once-royal gown to keep himself from tripping, the storyteller paused and blinked. Just ahead of him lay the crossing; and even with his bad eyes he could make out two tiny figures moving towards it from the west. Always curious, he shuffled on to meet them before their ways divided. But they moved much faster than he, and he was fairly panting with effort when he reached the crossroads as they approached to pass him by.

The storyteller experienced a sense of mild disappointment. From the distance he had received an impression of immense size and brightness; but now, under closer scrutiny, the two figures did not seem to him to be quite so unusual. One was a young man, tall and dark-haired. Though he was powerful-looking, there was nothing about him to set the storyteller's imagination alight. He carried neither sword nor dagger; his only weapon seemed to be a club of wild olive wood. He wore no sandals and consequently his feet were scratched and bloody; but nevertheless he was smiling rather proudly. He did not appear to notice the storyteller; his thoughts were plainly elsewhere. The other figure was that of a young woman. She, too, was smiling and a breath of intense happiness seemed to follow her like a perfume. Unlike the young man, she saw the storyteller; and her smile broadened into the beginnings of a laugh—as if the sight of the wrinkled old poet was suddenly comical. Indeed there was an air about her of finding everything comical and full of delight. She raised her hand in greeting; but the storyteller, offended, turned away. Then this strange, but not supernaturally strange pair had passed him by and were well on the way to Pherae.

For a long while he stood, staring after them; then he resumed his southward journey. As he did so, a faint sound reached him; it came from the direction of Pherae. He paused with his bald head on one side. Though his eyes might have been bad, his ears were still good; the sound was that of a distant, but tremendous shout of joy.

What had happened in Pherae? He shrugged his shoulders and wryly shook his head. He was too old and world-weary to change his direction now. Some day he would discover; some-where a simple servant or housekeeper would pluck him aside and, with bulging round eyes, tell him what he'd missed at Pherae and who had been brought back from the dead. He chuckled—and shook his wise old doubting head.

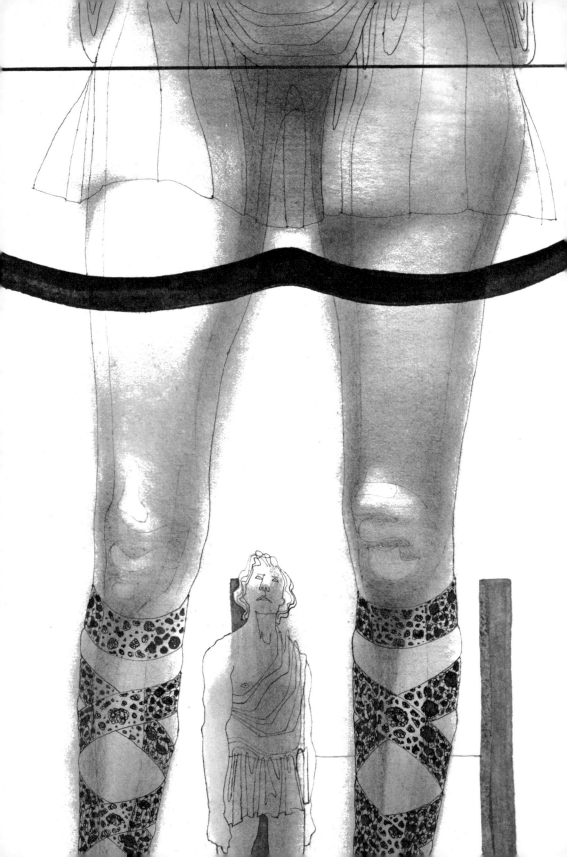

9 • Atalanta

So . . . the brand had been burned and Meleager was dead; the prophecy of the Fates had been fulfilled. The storyteller frowned and squinted at the sky; reason struggled with dreams, and he cursed his inquiring mind that would not let mystery be. Everywhere he'd heard wild tales of the hunting of the huge boar of Calydon; in Sparta, in Achaia and even in Pylus where he'd sung in the house of Nestor and been given a pair of sandals . . . but they were too large and hurt his feet, so he hung them round his neck and travelled by sea whenever he could.

What had really happened in the forest of Calydon; had the dark murders been plotted by men, not gods? These and other questions teased the old man's brain. What had become of the strange huntress who'd claimed to be the daughter of the King of Argos? She haunted his mind and he knew that, before he could do justice to the hunting of the Calydonian boar, he would need to know the fate of Atalanta.

He embarked on a vessel at Leuctra that took him—by way of calm seas and leisurely winds—to Lerna in Argolis and, ancient as he was, his heart quickened at the thought of beholding a woman believed by some to be Artemis, the huntress goddess herself.

Cautiously he skirted the swampy region to the east of Lerna where the malignant Hydra was said to lurk, until at last he came to Argos, to tell old stories and hear new ones. Truth to say, his present stock was growing threadbare; what with age cramping his fingers and wrinkling his voice, he stood in great need of novelty to earn his daily bread and nightly rest. Even Nestor's sandals and Peleus's robe would not keep out the weather for ever.

The grave fierce huntress had returned from Calydon; with

fair hair flying and brows drawn down, she had strode across the courtyard of the palace of Argos. She had mounted the steps and laid her bow and ivory quiver with its stock of arrows on an engraved bronze chest that stood within the entrance pillars.

The storyteller saw them as he shuffled by. The bow, tipped with golden horns, was unstrung; and the old man wondered if, even in his vigorous youth, he could have strung it. There were seven arrows remaining in the quiver; he drew one out and saw that its iron tip was beginning to rust. . . .

Though she had shed no tears, the memory of Meleager haunted her heart and mind, and the broken pain tormented her. Hour after hour she sat staring out of her casement towards the white shrine of Aphrodite that stood on a hillside beyond the courtyard walls. Her short cloak lay tumbled on the floor and her sandals beside it.

The storyteller knelt to touch them and turn them over in his rheumatic hands. Tiny pebbles were embedded in the soles and the inner part of the gilded thongs was worn almost flat. The old man ran his finger along them and the stout housekeeper, who stood over him, smiled. Though long since widowed, this good soul still contrived to keep some misty glimmer of love-light in her large dull eyes. . . .

But the King of Argos was a man of politics, treaties and alliances; though he knew as well as any the brief painful beauty of first love, he knew better than most the more painful necessities of the world. He had need of a grandson to secure his house. With all the sternness he could command, he bade Atalanta choose a husband without delay. There was no doubt that he thought his urgency and severity would shake his daughter from her silent mourning for Meleager. Certainly no unkindness had been meant; he was insanely proud of her and had had the huge boar tusks she had won in Calydon set above his throne. That very night he came to his daughter's chamber with some notion of softening his decree.

The room was bright with moonlight; she lay on her couch, still in her huntress's tunic. Her eyes were full of moon and anger. Her father approached and knelt beside her; he made as if to stroke her hair, but suddenly was almost afraid to raise his hand.

"Yes," she whispered without moving. "I will take a husband, if you will grant me one condition."

Eagerly the king nodded: the granting of a condition would ease the guilt he felt for his severity.

"Let whoever would have me, defeat me first in a race. But if he fails, then let him be—killed."

The king shrank back. He stared at his daughter whose beauty had become terrifying. It was like the beauty of Artemis herself; it trembled with the arrows of sudden death. Atalanta was as swift as the wind; no mortal could hope to defeat her. She closed her eyes, and her thoughts and dreams were hidden from her father for ever. . . .

The storyteller gazed down at the couch in the chamber; it seemed to bear an imprint even now. He bent low, almost as if to kiss it; then he straightened up. He had found a long golden hair. The housekeeper nodded, and the ancient man tucked it shamefacedly into his empty wallet. . . .

A wide, well-sanded path circled the palace courtyard where chariot races were sometimes held. Directly before the gates two posts had been set up and a thread stretched between them; this was to be the beginning and end of the race. A young man of Argos, much admired for his speed and good looks, had been persuaded by his friends to attempt to win Atalanta. Neither he nor they really believed that the grave-eyed girl would exact the terrible penalty if he lost; but at the same time no one doubted that the young man would claim his reward if he won.

She walked to the two posts dressed as if for a hunt; the young man looked at her long, slender legs bound to the knee with gold embroidered thongs; then his eyes met hers and his heart leaped with pride and passion. She smiled, and laid her bow and quiver beside the posts. The murmuring of the watching crowd died away; a chill swept through them. . . .

The king himself gave the signal; he flung a javelin. The young man's eyes followed it urgently and the instant it touched the ground he was away. He ran marvellously well—his golden legs ceaselessly reaching forward to fling the path behind him.

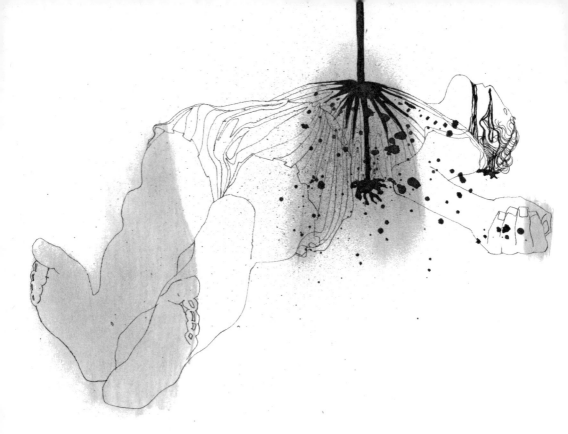

He felt full of speed and lightness; the wind danced in his hair and as he sped along the course a tapestry of faces unfolded and cheered him on to success.

For a while the girl ran beside him, keeping pace so exactly that each runner seemed a reflection of the other, their sandalled feet meeting the ground at the self-same moment and plucking up single blossoms of sand. Then—it was like a soul leaving its body; the double runner divided; she drew ahead so that the young man ran in her shadow; then that, too, left him and he ran alone. Briefly he saw her, seeming to fly out of his reach . . . then she rounded the curve of the path and was gone.

He smiled painfully, but nonetheless ran on, still encouraged by the cheering of his many friends. Then the cheering seemed to change to a sigh of dismay. Fear entered his heart. He reached the final curve that straightened into the end of the race.

She was waiting for him; she was standing between the posts, her bow in her hand. Carefully she notched an arrow; the sunlight glinted on its iron tip. He saw her right hand draw back till it caressed her cheek. Her eyes were grave and steady; the young man fancied he saw a gleam of pity in them . . . but this was only fancy. The arrow flew . . . he ran for a little way further; he seemed to be trying to smile and he pointed to the arrow in his chest as if he was proud of it. Then his legs burst into a frenzy; he looked suddenly ashamed—tried to hide his face . . . and fell dead.

A wind sprang up and ruffled the sand on the wide path. The storyteller stared at the two tall posts that flanked it; several strands of broken thread still fluttered from them. He held up his gown and shuffled along the path, kicking the sand as he went. He passed between the posts; the threads, if still stretched, would have cleared his shrivelled head. He peered at them, fingering their broken ends. . . .

"There were three more who ran . . ." muttered the house-keeper; and the old man gazed back along the path where ghost after ghost came slowly flying towards him, arms flung out, eyes imploring, meeting in mid-career the arrows of the grave-eyed girl who stood between the posts.

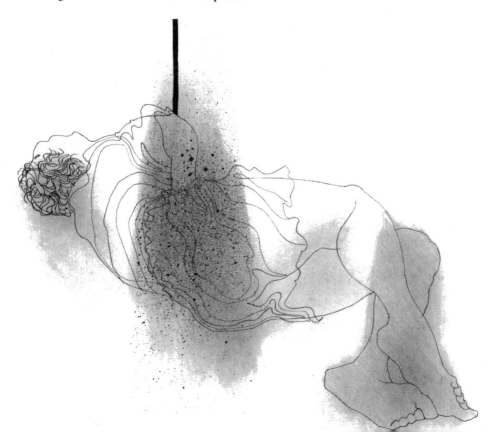

The crowds parted and the dead youths, their eyes and mouths filling up with sand, were dragged away. The watchers departed, leaving the silent girl to stare down at the empty sand where the marks of dying fingers were still plain.

She looked up, feeling instant eyes upon her. A solitary figure had remained behind; a youth with grey eyes very like her own. He was staring at her with a mixture of wonderment and defiance. He said nothing, but remained motionless so that she wondered if he was brother or close friend to the dead.

His image haunted her mind; his expression tantalised her. She could not put him out of her thoughts. He appeared again after the next race and stood watching her with the self-same expression. She was much taken aback—even though she had half expected to see him.

He came for a third time and stood, staring at her. She returned his look with its mirror image, but was unable to sustain it.

"What is your name?" she muttered.

"Melanion." Unaccountably he lingered on the first syllable so that she grew pale, thinking he was about to say "Meleager".

She returned to her chamber filled with a sense of angry foreboding. She stared out of her casement towards the shrine of Aphrodite on the hillside . . . and fancied she saw Melanion entering it. She looked away—and fancied she saw him vanishing among a clump of trees. She stared up to the sky—and saw his intent face swirling among the clouds; then she saw it composed in the crumpled linen of her couch. . . . Nor was he absent from her dreams: he, not she, stood between the posts with levelled arrow and grey, implacable eyes.

Sooner or later she knew he would be her opponent in the contest, and she half-longed for the day and half-dreaded it. Yet when the day came and she saw him crouching in readiness, all her haunting thoughts rose up within her and she fancied the race itself was but a continuation of her dreams.

With hands that trembled she laid her bow and quiver beside the posts and took up her place.

"Why?" she murmured to the youth she must destroy.

"Because I love you, Atalanta."

"I will kill you."

"Perhaps."

"Think again."

"I have."

"Then have you prayed, Melanion?"

"Only to the goddess of love."

The javelin flew and struck the ground; the race had begun. As before, the girl kept pace with the youth exactly, seeming to take a delight in matching her stride and watching her opponent's straining face. He scowled as he ran and seemed to have some awkwardness with his clenched fists.

On one side the palace walls rushed by her: on the other, the never-ending crowd. She saw their eager faces, greedily waiting for the beginning of the end.

"Farewell, Melanion," she whispered, and drew ahead. She could hear him breathing harshly as he made a frantic effort to increase his pace. Helplessly she strained her ears to listen for any word, but the huge roaring of the crowd filled her head and made it sing.

Suddenly something danced and glittered in her path. It leaped and bounced, catching the sun with little golden explosions. What was it? She paused. It was an apple—an apple

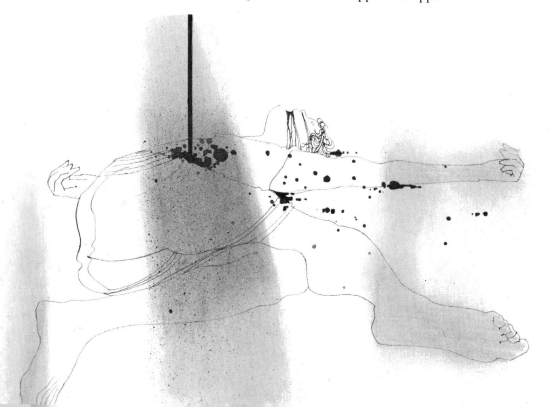

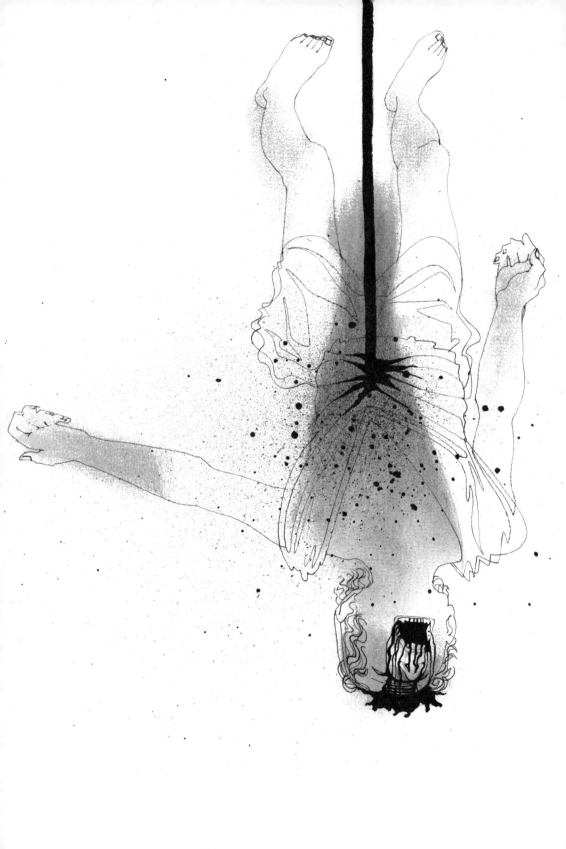

made of gold. Fascinated, she stooped and gathered it up . . . and Melanion sped panting past her. She laughed, tucked the golden apple into the folds of her tunic and overtook him as easily as if his pace had been no swifter than a walk.

Once more she ran beside him and watched his face all carved with the agony of effort. "Melanion—Melanion—" she murmured, and lingered by him to catch a reply. But the roaring of the crowd had grown louder and the two runners seemed like spirits speeding silently through a storm.

Then Atalanta wearied of tantalising the youth; she seemed almost to drift ahead of him—as if he and she were fixed in different worlds, each turning its own way. Then again something golden leaped and bounded in her path. She hesitated, glanced from side to side and then to the sweep of the course before her. So long was Melanion's life; she smiled; she would stretch it out a little. She stooped for the second golden apple . . . and once more Melanion stumbled past her, his lips drawn back and his teeth clenched as if to prevent his life escaping with his anguished breath.

How many more golden apples had he to tempt her from the race? She overtook him with an ease that made the crowd groan.

"Melanion . . . Melanion . . ." she whispered again as she bore him company towards his death. His chin was streaked with blood where he'd bitten into his lips. She saw his mouth open— and she stayed her increasing pace to hear him. The noise of the crowd had grown in pitch to a howling of excitement. His lips moved and moved; desperately she longed to hear him before it was too late. In her mind's eye she saw him flying towards her— and her arrow racing to meet him and cut off his words for ever.

"The last one!" he panted. "Take it, Atalanta!"

The third golden apple fell from Melanion's despairing hand.

"Is that all, Melanion?" sighed Atalanta. "Have you nothing more to say to me?"

She watched his face, his lips, his racing hair and staring eyes as they moved beside her . . . then she gathered up the third golden apple from out of Melanion's shadow as he flung himself onward into the endless sweeping curve of the course, down which Atalanta's dream arrow was already flying.

For a moment she paused to watch his stumbling figure; she

saw his footprints twisting and weaving in the tumbled sand. Then she heard the crowd screaming in anticipation—and she sped away for the third and last time.

A silence fell on the multitude; they looked on in helpless dread. Atalanta's face, set in the streaming amazement of her hair, was the grave implacable face of Artemis, goddess of sudden death.

The rushing wind painted her tunic against her breasts and flying thighs . . . she laughed aloud; she and the inquisitive air were one. She was a spirit—a dream in men's minds to be possessed only in sleep and death.

She looked up; Melanion was no more than an arm's length before her.

"Alas, Melanion, have you no more golden apples?"

"All the apples of the Hesperides, Atalanta," he shouted; "now you are mine!"

Even as he answered, a shadow fell across his back; he had passed between the posts and snapped the thread! Atalanta's heart leaped with bewilderment and terror. She had misjudged the distance; she had lost the race!

"To be possessed only in sleep and death," muttered the story-teller.

"Only in sleep . . . and death," echoed the housekeeper, the love-light in her large dull eyes spreading like a cataract.

She ran from Melanion across the fields that sloped away towards the river; then she turned sharply and mounted the hillside to the pillared shrine of Aphrodite. He pursued, wondering if she would seek sanctuary from him. She paused, glanced back towards the distant walls of the palace and the casement from which she had so often looked out, then vanished within the shrine.

With fierce excitement he followed her and entered the mysterious, circular temple. Pillars surrounded him: tall, cool, like huge, blind, whitened nymphs. The statue of the goddess was seated before her altar; Atalanta crouched in her lap.

"Meleager," she whispered; "Meleager—come to me."

"I am Melanion—" he muttered . . . and their low voices

ran round the pillars like mice.

"Meleager . . . Melanion—come to me. . . ."

She stretched out her hands. Her grey eyes glimmered in the dim light; amber fires seemed to be kindled in them.

"This is a holy place . . ." whispered Melanion.

"This is a holy place," echoed Atalanta mockingly—and opened wide her arms. "Come to me. . . ."

"Would you defile the altar, Atalanta?"

"Would you not defile the—altar, Melanion?"

"The goddess will take her revenge, Atalanta. . . ."

"The goddess has taken her revenge," whispered Atalanta as her lover embraced her in the very lap of the goddess. "See, my love. . . ."

He stared down into her eyes; the amber fires had quite consumed them. He snarled and backed away. She rose angrily and leaped down on to the floor. He followed, padding softly and shaking his head from side to side. She uttered a strange low cry—and slunk out between the pillars. He bounded in her wake; then they sped down the hillside, she outdistancing him and howling as she ran. Then he, in some savage passion, whined and roared till their two voices echoed and re-echoed in the evening air. . . .

"Lions," mumbled the housekeeper. "They were changed into lions for their sin."

The old man touched the cold columns of the shrine and blinked mistily down at the scratched floor. The air smelled damp and earthy, and the huge stone face of the goddess oppressed him with thoughts of death. He stumbled out and looked across the wide landscape. Sunset clouds rolled in a slow blaze across distant hills. He saw a pair of lions among them, harnessed by flying streamers to a loosely woven chariot; then, as he watched, the streamers broke away, the chariot dissolved and holes appeared in the lions, changing them into stags, then hounds, then bounding runners, speeding dreamingly through a sky of golden apples. . . .

The old man sighed and opened his wallet. He took out the long, golden hair, held it for a moment between his fingers, then let it fall and vanish on the evening breeze. . . .

10 • Snakes in the Courtyard

The quiet sand, the rocky promontory and the fisherman's boat—once scarlet but now flaked and faded to a whisper of red—tantalised the old man's mind. Had he been there before, or had he heard of something like it and woven it into a tale? He shook his head and seated himself in the shadow of the boat. Nowadays it was hard to distinguish between memory and imagination. Far, far to the south—at the other end of winter—lay the palace of Argos, haunted by Atalanta . . . if ever there was such a woman of flesh and blood. Yet he'd touched her bow and quiver, held her sandals; he opened his wallet and fumbled inside . . . he sighed. Not so much as a hair of her remained.

What was the real truth of it all? Housekeepers' tales and his own longing for the world to be larger and more mysterious than it was. However brightly everything shone in his mind, in his hands it crumbled to dust.

Northward lay Iolcus where Peleus had fled after he had killed Eurytion in the forest of Calydon. Peleus, the great hero flawed with envy. . . . The old man drowsily fingered the tatters of his gown, and tried to imagine a young man mighty enough to have filled it out. The sun dropped down; the shadows spread and the sea darkened. Again the familiarity of the place swept through him, producing a curious sensation of dreamy excitement. He felt that he was on the very edge of remembering something extraordinarily important. He struggled to keep awake; the memory was almost within his grasp. He frowned at the promontory—now black and uncanny. He remembered—he remembered—

"Who will my lover be?"

The sea whispered, the myrtle bushes that screened an opening in the rocks shivered and seemed to bend aside. The dark air was full of shapes, not solid but of the air itself, that rolled soundlessly round the old man's sleeping head. His lips moved; his face broke into a million wrinkles that did service as a smile.

"Thetis!" he mumbled, remembering everything now. "Thetis, the sea goddess . . . sandals of silver ferns. . . ."

"My lover . . . my lover . . ." whispered the voice over the sleeping storyteller's head. Eyes brushed across him as if he'd been no more than a stone.

The sea stirred and rippled; waves came rapidly, sighing and panting on the shore.

"Thetis, my love—"

"Who is there?"

"Poseidon, Lord of the Sea."

"How will you love me?"

"With storms and calms; with waves and whirlpools and golden waterspouts—"

"Will you give me a son, Poseidon?"

The old man, lying in the shadow of the fisherman's boat, mumbled again in his sleep as memories came flooding back.

"The son of Thetis will surpass his father."

"A son, Poseidon; will you give me a son?"

But the waves retreated; the sea flattened and crept away. Poseidon was a jealous god.

Shadows darkened the sleeping storyteller; then the myrtles bent aside once more. Other eyes stared down on the curious scene, remote eyes, full of pain and ice . . . yet not without humour; they observed the shrunken little figure snoring by the long-forgotten boat while enormous politics juggled above his head. Prometheus, unravelling the design of his dream of freedom, marvelled at little things falling into place and supporting a pattern too large to be seen. Who was moving whom, the Titan wondered?

The old man fidgeted, scratched himself and turned over as if to burrow into the sand and hide himself from some disturbing dream.

"Who will my lover be?"

Zeus stirred restively in the sky. Thoughts of mankind faded from Prometheus's mind. He watched the sky—and the quiet

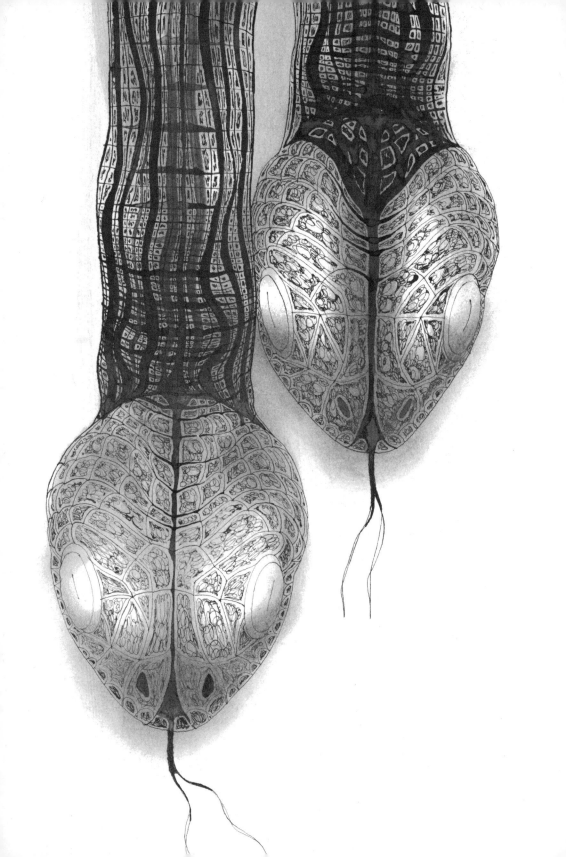

myrtles on the Thessalian shore.

"The son of Thetis will surpass his father," mumbled the old man, but into the extinguishing sand.

Suddenly something moved; a puffy, speckled snake, disturbed by the old man's mumblings and scrapings, wriggled out of the sand and began to crawl across his neck.

"Heracles has a mighty enemy!" shouted the storyteller, jerking bolt upright, but still asleep. The touch of the snake had driven away his dream and replaced it with another. He seized the venomous reptile and squeezed its neck.

"Hera sends serpents to destroy him!"

The young man with the wild olive club and clear grey eyes, seemed to dance rather than walk as he left Pherae for his home in Thebes. The world was a fine place; the sun shone and the young man strolled and ran, sleeping under the stars—for he liked nothing between him and the heavens—and eating simply and even humbly in any cottage where the smell of roast meat drew him from the road. Children especially delighted him and he loitered in sleepy villages to teach wide-eyed youngsters how to use a bow and arrow, but more for the pleasure of their admiration of his own skill, it must be admitted, than with any thoughts of fitting them for war.

"Say Heracles taught you!" he'd laugh as he tried to escape from their eager hands and flattering cries for more.

"What? Would you pull Heracles down?"

"Are you really Heracles?"

"Heracles of Thebes."

"Are you really as strong as they say?"

The young man would look serious and doubting; he'd pick up a child, straining under its tiny weight; then, with a shout of triumph, he'd toss the child so high in the air that it must have seen the world spinning before falling, gasping and laughing, into Heracles's sure arms. Then, leaving the child safely on its feet, he'd chuckle and cry, "Enough! I've four sons of my own who are waiting to be thrown to the skies!"

Sometimes he'd pass through villages where loud-mouthed local champions made it their business to challenge peaceful travellers—and send them sprawling in the dust. These men, all

scowls and muscles and necks as thick as trees, both fascinated
and alarmed the young man. With modest smiles he'd decline
the combat, plead haste—or anything to avoid it. He was no
wrestler—he was quite sure he'd be defeated—he was almost
frightened by men so deft and strong. But they would insist—
these jeering local heroes—for the young man seemed to tempt
them so; and then they'd find themselves most mysteriously flat
upon their backs with the young man gazing inoffensively down
upon them. When they made to rise, he'd ease them back with his
foot and smilingly console them with:

"Say Heracles threw you. It's no disgrace to have been beaten
by Heracles of Thebes; he has wrestled with the god of death—
and won!"

The memory of his victory on the road to Aornum was
never far from Heracles's thoughts. He had achieved what no
mortal had ever done; he had torn a woman from the dusty,
suffocating arms of death and restored her to the world once
more.

Amazement, pride and joy never ceased to fill him as he remembered. His ears still rang with the mighty shout of happiness
when he'd returned to the palace of Pherae, leading Alcestis by
the hand. "My lord Admetus," he'd said, having prepared a
long and grand address; then tears had flooded his eyes and
reduced his eloquence to: "Here is your wife."

"You are a tremendous hero, Heracles of Thebes," he'd
mumble, and beam at his reflection in the streams where he
bathed; then he'd look round sheepishly—to make sure he hadn't
been overheard. Though he admired modesty and always strove
to cultivate it, in his heart of hearts he found it hard not to be
enormously proud of what he'd done.

He found it particularly hard to be modest whenever he
thought of his cousin, the King of Mycenae. Scarcely a day separated them in age; yet because Eurystheus of Mycenae had the
advantage of that day, he was lord of the House of Perseus and
Heracles owed him allegiance. He was mean, contemptible and
unworthy in everything except birth; yet Heracles must needs
bow to him and call him "Lord". Though Heracles did his best
to conceal his opinions, it was perfectly plain that Eurystheus was
aware that his great cousin despised him and he took a malicious
pleasure in observing Heracles's strenuous attempts at respect.

"If only it had been you, Eurystheus, in the arms of death," muttered Heracles, momentarily depressed; then he sighed and gave a rueful smile. Strong as he was, he was not strong enough to carry the burden of hatred to the gates of the grave. He lacked the inward iron. He knew he would have fought to save his cousin even as he'd saved Alcestis.

At the thought of Alcestis his spirits rose and he continued on his light-hearted way to Thebes, taking comfort, when he needed it, from picturing his four noisy sons who, one day, would be kings and have a better father to boast of than would the virtuous children of Mycenae.

His heart swelled to bursting as he anticipated his return to Thebes; already he could see the bright eyes and open mouths as he related his adventures in such a bed-time tale as would never be heard in the house of Eurystheus. At least, he didn't have to be modest with his beloved sons!

The sky was clear, the sun was blazing as he entered the gates of the palace at Thebes. He raised his finger to his lips to silence the guards who would have shouted and clashed their ironmongery in welcome. He wanted to surprise his children—to burst upon them with a godlike radiance.

They would be in the courtyard at the back of the palace where he'd built them a small parade ground to play at soldiers and command such of the palace children who would still take orders from captains with squeaky voices.

He walked lightly and rapidly along the front colonnade; already he could hear orders shouted, orders disagreed with, orders flatly contradicted—at the very tops of high voices. He smiled and quickened his pace.

Suddenly he paused. Some drops of warmish rain had fallen on his head. He looked up; the sky was still clear. Vague, disquieting memories troubled him. Two further drops fell, splashing in his eyes. For a moment he was blinded, seeing only tiny silver snakes wriggling down his sight. He wiped his eyes and walked on.

The sound of voices had died. There was an airless silence that seemed curiously threatening. What had happened? Fear entered the father's heart; he tightened his grip on his club. He ran towards where his children were; he had heard a hissing sound as of fire catching damp wood. At first he thought it was inside his head, but it grew louder and more distinct.

He reached the little courtyard—and cried out in dread and disgust. Writhing in the summer's dust was a knot of puffy, speckled snakes. As if to greet him, scaly poisonous heads lifted out of the menacing turmoil, swayed at him and put out little black tongues. . . .

Dread gave way to anger and hatred. He ran forward and, lifting his club, brought it smashing down on the struggling reptiles. Hissing with pain, they scattered; then one by one he seized them by their quick tails and dashed their yawning heads against the ground . . . again and again until they squirmed no more. At last they lay, twisted and broken about the courtyard. There had been eight of them.

As in a dream, he went to fetch wood to light a fire and burn the dead snakes. He passed two servants who stared at him and fled. He saw no one else. He gathered several logs and carried them back quickly; he was anxious to rid the place of the venomous remains.

He entered the courtyard once more. There were no snakes there. Instead there were eight dead children. Four were the sons of Heracles; the others had been their companions. They lay twisted and broken as if by the hand of a madman.

Heracles dropped the wood he had been carrying. He stared down at his hands; they were bright with blood. He raised his eyes to the sky, and screamed. It was he who had been the madman.

11 ● A Lion Hunt

There was a darkness in the palace of Thebes; the casements were shut and the doors swung listlessly on their hinges. The servants were gone and with them the mistress of the house, huge-eyed with terror and grief. From time to time a movement in the air caused the ashes in the fireplaces to whisper and rise like phantoms; then they settled and all was stillness again. Sometimes there were footsteps—shuffling, dragging footsteps that moved from dark room to dark room; then they ceased and there was a sound of harsh weeping intermingled with words such as might be uttered to children.

Such noises, which continued for five nights and days, were like the hopeless grieving of a ghost. Then this ghost came out. Bent-shouldered, sunken-eyed and with savage marks on his cheeks and breast, made by knives or finger-nails, Heracles departed from Thebes. As he walked, he stared at the ground; he could not bear to look on any living soul—and no living soul could bear to look on him.

He took the road on which he had travelled so short a time before; but the journey now was different. He skirted the villages and ran from the sight and sound of children with his hands clapped to his ears; their laughing voices entered his brain like arrows. He bathed by night, when darkness would hide the reflection of the madman's face; he dreaded it would look no different, no less gentle, no less kind than the face of any father. . . .

Once he tried to hang himself from a snaky willow branch, but the thought of meeting with the ghosts of his murdered children caused him to shrink from the relief of suicide. He knew that to meet peacefully with those he had killed he must needs come with such a dowry of suffering that not ten lifetimes could amass.

So he walked and walked with no other purpose, it seemed, than to exhaust his bewildered mind. Yet all the while there was something deep in his spirit that would not be quenched and which led him to the one place on earth where even he might be helped.

He came to it early one morning, a steep, quiet place between wooded mountains. Poised amid the dark trees above him was a shrine, a colonnaded nest for flying gods. He had reached Delphi, and before him was the temple of Apollo.

He crouched in the stunted grass, remaining motionless for many hours, while he summoned up courage to enter the temple and beg such a punishment from the gods that would balance out the horror of his crime. By now his anguish had lost some of its sharpness and sunk to a dull, leaden ache which his cramped position seemed to ease.

Little by little he became absorbed in a small patch of ground where a nation of insects were toppling hither and thither, bearing tiny boulders of dust to raise walls, palaces and temples in a country an arm's length off. He fell to wondering if they could see his huge face, and if his eyes were their grey skies with two black suns glaring down? Was this a great occasion for them, to be remembered for generations? Perhaps even now they were praying to him to be forgiven their insect sins. Great Face, what must we do to atone? Shall we catch a huge fierce bee and offer it up to you? Shall we build you a temple as high as the tallest blade of grass?

At last, Heracles rose; he was ready to enter the temple and learn his punishment. His state was dream-like; he scarcely saw the priestess who greeted him as a son of Zeus. He sighed; much good the divine seed had done him. Perhaps, even, it was the conflict between his divine and mortal parts that had made him mad?

"What must I do?"

"Leave Thebes, Heracles. Go to Mycenae and serve Eurystheus. Do whatever he bids you."

Heracles bowed his head. There had been a time when such a command would have filled him with anger and shame and seemed the end of the world; but now it was ant-like in proportion to his guilt.

The priestess spoke again. "He will set you twelve labours,

Heracles. These you must endure."

"What labours can such a man as Eurystheus devise that would purify me of my crime? What can his spirit know of mine?"

But to this there was no answer and Heracles left the temple of Apollo as sombrely as he had entered it. He turned his steps towards Mycenae and the beginning of his Labours.

The King of Mycenae was a man of taste; the very set of his lips and the slight but continual working of his mouth suggested he was always tasting—and hadn't really made up his mind whether anything was good or bad. Not even his wife escaped this cultured, critical air of his; consequently she wore a tight-lipped smile that suggested she had even more refined opinions of her own.

"So, Heracles, the gods have chosen me to decide upon your punishment." Eurystheus, seated high, gazed down on the young man the gods had delivered into his hands. Travel-stained and smeared with grief, Heracles returned his cousin's look, then lowered his eyes.

"Twelve labours you are to set me, Lord Eurystheus. . . ."

The king's mouth worked meditatively as he savoured the pleasure of his situation; while the queen beside him smiled her tight-lipped smile at the bronze floor, the rich hangings, the absorbed servants and her own neat hands.

"He must be kept from children," said this queen, who, above all things, desired to show that she thought of matters her husband might have overlooked. Heracles's eyes blazed with sudden tears; the queen nodded with satisfaction; she had drawn first blood.

"You are strong, Heracles," said Eurystheus, with a knowledgeable, considered air, "and we must make clever use of your strength, eh? And you have experience in, for want of a better word shall we say, murdering? So I would have you murder something for me, Heracles. But not a child, or a teacher; you have already shown how easily you can manage that . . . hm?"

Eurystheus paused; he watched the young man with refined curiosity—as if he was observing some rare species of insect writhing in interesting pain.

"Yes. I would have you kill the great lion of Nemea, Heracles."

He smiled. "Thus one pest shall rid the world of another, eh? And who cares which butchers which!"

"And the skin," put in the queen. "Let him flay the lion and bring back the skin. Else how shall we know whose blood is on his hands?"

The King of Mycenae glanced at his wife; and for once there was a cautious admiration in his eyes.

"Goodbye, Heracles. May the gods go with you . . . for assuredly you need watching, eh?"

Exiled from Thebes, Heracles now lived in Tiryns, an obscure town to the south of Mycenae. Thither he returned to put his affairs in order before setting out on an enterprise from which he might not return. Then, taking with him the sword and quiver of arrows given him by Alcmena, his mother, and said to have been made by the gods, he set out for the mountains of Nemea.

These mountains lay scarcely two days' journey to the north, yet Heracles contrived to fill the brief distance with all the thoughts, musings and leave-takings that stretch from heaven to hell. Every tree, stream, sleeping shepherd set off a thousand dreams and memories . . . some of his past life, some of his mysterious origins and his miraculous babyhood. He remembered Amphitryon, his mother's husband who was said not to have been his father and was now dead upon some battlefield. Amphitryon haunted him with his half-admiring, half-angry looks. . . . Then, as the countryside grew mountainous, his thoughts turned more and more to what lay ahead.

The Lion of Nemea. Was there such a beast, or was it just an idea in men's minds: a figure of speech, almost, for something too monstrous to exist outside of nightmares? Said to have been born of the mating of a goddess with a giant, it was called a lion because of its strength and savagery; but there all likeness to any earthly creature ceased. Its hide was believed to be proof against all weapons and its breath as foul and poisonous as the Lernian Hydra's. Tales of the lion had been abroad as long as Heracles himself; he could just remember an old nurse, her eyes deep and her mouth shuddering, trying to frighten him off to bed with threats of the Nemean lion.

"Huge, twitchy thing with eyes as red as blood and a mouthful of knives for teeth! He creeps through doors and windows to gobble up children out of bed!"

"Have you—seen it?"

"No! The gods forbid!"

"Then who—?"

"I knew a man whose brother had been eaten up. Nought but his eyes remained—and they stared and stared from a puddle in the rocks. Horrible. . . ."

"Because he was out of bed?"

The nurse had nodded; and Heracles began to wonder, as he mounted higher and higher into rocky Nemea, whether he had been set to kill a dream fear and bring back its skin. Presently, towards evening on the second day, he reached level ground. He paused, shielding his eyes against the sudden glare of the setting sun. He could just make out the walls of Nemea itself; with brisk walking he would reach the town before nightfall. He set off again, but discovered he had misjudged the distance. The town was still an hour away when darkness invaded the sky and swallowed up the landmarks.

"He creeps through doors and windows to gobble up children out of bed." The words of his old nurse echoed in his mind and again he wondered whether he was hunting a shadow he could never kill—and which could never kill him?

"Where are you?" he whispered; and the night breezes sighed and moaned through invisible bushes like a frightened man's imaginings of a roaring lion. Lion-shaped shadows quivered in pools of rock—but never sprang; his own footfalls seemed to pad in his wake—but never caught him up. Little by little a terrible emptiness entered his spirit. If there was no lion, there was no punishment; if there was no punishment, there was no peace for his soul. Dully he roamed the wild and forlorn place until at last he saw a faint sprinkling of brightness amid a clump of trees. He hastened towards it and discovered it to be coming from a cottage, much patched against the weather and leaking light at every joint. Eagerly he knocked and, after a lengthy pause, there came a voice from within: "Molorchus is here. Who wants him?"

"A stranger," answered Heracles. "Will you give me shelter?"

"You have been looking for me, then?"

"No; I saw your light. I am a stranger—"

"But you know of me? You know the name . . . Molorchus?"

"I am not from these parts. I have come a long way—"

"—to see Molorchus!"

The door opened and a smallish, square-built man peered first at Heracles's chest and then upward to his troubled grey eyes.

"I can offer you nothing but barley cakes," said Molorchus apologetically. "As you must know, my wife has gone and I'm quite alone."

Heracles looked about him, and as he did so his heart leaped with hope. Though the cottage was clean, it was by no means tidy. A great number of enterprises lay unfinished everywhere. Half-carved pieces of wood, half-chiselled stones and many urns and pots partly painted and put aside. Lions were in all of them; just begun, ghostly lions lacking legs, or eyes, or tails. Molorchus in his loneliness had been occupying himself.

"Then there *is* a lion of Nemea!" breathed Heracles, his eyes ranging the desperate lions of Molorchus's brain; poor as they were, they seemed like the phantom tracks of the great beast himself through the air of the cottage. Somehow the creature had brushed against this man and left its scent across his life.

"It's the fierceness I can't get," said Molorchus, who never stopped talking. As with all men who live alone, his thoughts and very soul itself came out with a rush to greet the merest chance companion. He flew from bench to bench, picking up carving after carving and demonstrating where each had failed in this or that particular. He seemed almost proud of having missed his aim; it was as if his very failure flattered his taste.

"Then you have seen the lion?" said Heracles, while Molorchus drew breath.

"No; not I. To see it is to die by it, sir. No one sees it and lives, you know."

"Then all these—" Heracles indicated the stillborn monsters.

"My special connection, you understand. Surely you know— you must have heard that my son was killed by the lion?" Molorchus blinked up at Heracles with the shy and mournful pride of the bereaved. . . . "It was quite famous. I was sick that day, so my son went out with the herds. And the Nemean lion destroyed him. For some reason known only to themselves the gods wanted me to be preserved. Many people came, you know, to mourn with me; important men from the city, even. My wife made barley cakes and they drank wine right here in this cottage. It was a great occasion. . . ."

As Heracles listened with weary courtesy, he began to see himself mirrored in this little man who was so inflated with grief and guilt that nothing existed outside of his own tragedy. Hoping to stem the tide of chatter, Heracles told Molorchus who he was. Molorchus nodded; he had heard of Heracles . . . he recalled having heard something about Zeus and Alcmena from an old storyteller—and a tale of serpents strangled in a cradle; but beyond that he knew nothing, and Heracles perceived ruefully that Molorchus wasn't particularly interested.

"I have come to Nemea to kill your lion, Molorchus."

At once the tide was stemmed. In the middle of a word Molorchus fell silent. He peered at Heracles incredulously; then a pathetic resentment crept round the corners of his mouth. This stranger, this tall Heracles was come to destroy the greatest thing in Molorchus's life.

"No," he whispered. "No one can kill it. Its hide is proof against all weapons, sir. That's certain, you know. It's you who will be killed. Don't go, Heracles. Please. . . ."

"I must, Molorchus," murmured Heracles, striving by the gentleness of his voice to comfort Molorchus; for he pitied this man who had never escaped from his tragedy more, even, than he pitied himself. "It is the will of the gods."

"The gods?" cried Molorchus, brightening up. "Then the gods must have sent you to me! Yes; I see it now: you, me and the terrible lion! It is a very great occasion, sir. But you will be killed, you know; and once more it will be Molorchus preserved to tell the tale and keep it bright."

"I will go at dawn, Molorchus. If, after thirty days, I have not come back, pray for my soul in Hades—for that's where it will be. But if I came back, you and I will pray to Zeus together, Molorchus. . . ."

The days hung heavily on Molorchus; each one seemed like four or five. After a week it seemed impossible that a month had not passed and that Heracles's ghost was not already fading for want of prayers. Dazedly Molorchus caught himself wondering if he really wanted Heracles to return. Hastily he pushed the question to the back of his mind, but was unable to keep from counting the days with guilty eagerness. Confusion reigned in his thoughts; so, to calm himself, he set about carving yet another lion as fierce and horrible and huge as only a frightened man could make it.

For Heracles also the days hung heavily. The mountains of Nemea were harsh and blazing in the sun—and cold as death under the moon. Only twice in all the days of his searching did Heracles see so much as a living creature. He saw a goat leaping across high rocks and he saw what seemed to be a ragged-coated panther bounding across a piece of open ground.

He made no attempt to bring either of them down; he had not been hungry nor had the creatures threatened him in any way. But as the days wore on he came to regret his magnanimity; his store of food declined and the constant sunlight played tricks with his sight so that he feared he would lose the sureness of his aim. Consequently he took to loosing arrows at tree-trunks and bushes, transfixing particular leaves and even dividing twigs, and he returned over and over again to the places where he'd seen the goat and the ragged-coated panther-like beast. He never saw the goat again, but he glimpsed the other creature on two separate occasions. The first of these was towards nightfall when he dared not chance an arrow for fear of missing and frightening the creature from its regular haunts altogether; but the second time he saw it was in the early morning when the light was faultless. It was padding across the same stretch of open ground some way below. It was carrying something in its mouth that dripped, but the distance was too great to make out what the creature had scavenged and was now bearing off to its lair.

Cautiously Heracles moved down among the rocks to where they formed a line of natural battlements interrupted by narrow embrasures. Here he settled himself against the hot stone, with an arrow notched and his bow bent till it grunted in his clenched hand.

He waited, staring along the line of the arrow to where its bronze head ranged the ground that lay in the animal's path. It came into view quite slowly, moving across the narrow line of vision afforded by the embrasure and shaking its head from side

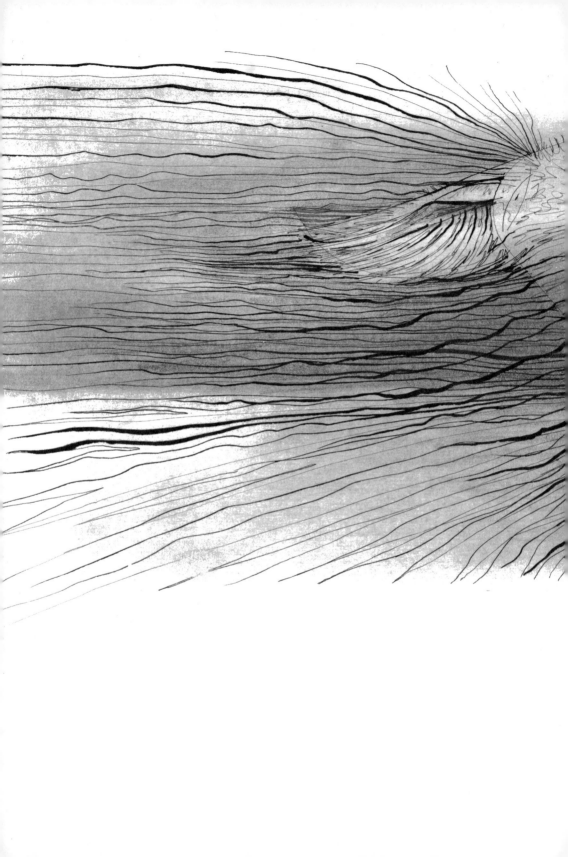

to side as if to toss the blood out of the limp creature it was carrying.

Carefully and coldly Heracles observed the folding and unfolding of the ragged-coated beast's shoulders and marked the fatal spot between them with the steadily-moving arrowhead. He waited till the creature should pause, as it frequently did, to gain a better grip on its bulky prey.

As if by design, it halted directly below him; at once the bowstring hummed and flashed and the arrow raced down, its feathers whirling like a bird of death. It struck the beast precisely between its shoulders; then the shaft snapped and the bronze head fell uselessly to the ground.

Slowly the creature raised its head and gazed up at the rocks. Huge golden eyes met those of Heracles; and a face, framed by a ragged mane, that was ancient and bewilderingly sad, as if there was no pleasure in being a bringer of death. Then it bent once more to take up the full-grown cow it had been carrying as if it had been no more than a newborn calf.

Once more the naked landscape of Nemea had deceived Heracles into misjudging size and distance. The beast below him was gigantic; it was the lion of Nemea.

A high, tragic excitement filled the young man as he stared down on the first of his Labours. Fear, amazement and an extraordinary relief struggled in his heart. "No one sees it and lives." But how many had seen it even as he'd seen it before and•not known what they'd seen . . . and so lived on to dream of something worse? Here was a great mystery, and Heracles was curiously reminded of what the blind seer Teiresias had told him long ago about a storyteller searching for the gods as if all creation was a game of hide-and-seek. How many heroes, gods and marvels that journeying man must have seen and lived never to tell the tale?

But now the huge lion had begun to move off, still shaking its head as if it was troubled by grim thoughts. Quietly Heracles laid aside his god-fashioned sword and arrows and descended from the security of the rocks. Then, with rapid, silent strides, he followed after the monster, his only weapons now being those he had come into the world with—his bare hands; for the iron-skinned lion of Nemea was proof against all else.

Hideous beyond reason, beyond belief, the lion gaped with a mouthful of knives for teeth. Had it ever thought to shut its mouth it would surely have sliced its face off; but it was fixed and stony, being the latest work of Molorchus.

He had worked like a madman in order to make the days speed by, already his heart had counted a hundred, though the sun had scarcely finished with twenty-nine. This new lion—the first he had ever completed—would serve as a funeral monument. People would come—great ones this time—to pay their respects and break barley cakes with Molorchus who was the last to see Heracles alive. . . .

As the thought occurred, he returned to his last lion and began contemplating it so proudly that he did not hear the door open or the step behind him.

"No, Molorchus. Its fierceness was not like that."

Heracles had come back. Molorchus trembled; then, straightening his shoulders, he prepared himself to endure the great young man's triumph. He turned; and his resentful heart misgave him. The young man stood with outstretched arms, as if in supplication. Molorchus observed that in place of one finger on his left hand there was a crusted flower of blood. So much the lion of Nemea had cost him.

"The lion is dead now. I followed it to its cave and there I strangled it. Come, Molorchus, we must pray to Zeus. We must thank him for—for being alive in the world. . . ."

He took Molorchus by the hand and together they went outside the cottage into the quiet night where they knelt, side by side, and prayed to the watchful stars.

"I have made fresh barley cakes," muttered Molorchus, when they rose again. "Will you break them with me, Heracles? This is a great occasion indeed, sir. . . ."

Heracles remained with Molorchus until the morning and then he departed from the alien mountains, sometimes dragging, sometimes carrying across his shoulders the limp, monstrous lion of Nemea.

For a while, Molorchus watched him, toiling under his burden on his way to Mycenae; then he sighed, bolted his cottage door and departed also, carrying his stone lion down into the world with the tale of Heracles and that great occasion when, side by side, they prayed to Zeus and broke barley cakes together.

12 • The Deadliest Snake of All

For the first time since his madness and the murdering of his children, Heracles smiled. It was not a broad smile, nor yet a very gay one; it was wry, and forced from him by Eurystheus, King of Mycenae, who had bolted at the very sight of the dead lion and issued panic-stricken orders that henceforth the fruits of Heracles's Labours should be displayed *outside* the palace gates. The news of this smile reached Eurystheus and increased his dislike of Heracles; however it did not cause him to abandon certain works that were going on in the palace. A circular chamber, rather like a large pot, was being constructed underground out of heavy bronze and it was his intention to retire into this whenever the return of his hated cousin should be signalled. Unhappily Eurystheus had a great distaste—amounting almost to a terror—for the sight of blood. This weakness, which he freely admitted to being a consequence of his extreme refinement, gave his queen a distinct advantage over him, which showed itself in a tight-lipped smile of more than ordinary dimensions. Thus with smiles to the left of him and smiles to the right of him, Eurystheus could not wait to get into his underground pot and defy the world from there.

"And have we decided on the Second Labour, my lord?"

The Queen of Mycenae peered down into the half-finished refuge. Eurystheus stared up. His eyes met his wife's. He raised his hands to either side of his head and waved them sinuously. The queen nodded; her smile broadened.

"Of course! Exactly my own idea. I will send a messenger to tell him what he must do now."

A fair-sized crowd was gathered outside the palace gates where Heracles had stretched out the dead Nemean lion and was puzzling how to flay it, for even in death the creature's hide was proof against every blade. Advice was being freely offered, and in particular Heracles found himself plagued by a boy of about thirteen, Iolaus by name, who owned a very splendid knife that had been given him for his birthday. Iolaus was absolutely certain that nothing was proof against his knife, which he had sharpened to an unbelievable edge; indeed, various parts of his home bore testimony to its excellence. He kept urging it on Heracles, even resorting to jibes and jeers to sting the hero into trying it.

"Go home, child," sighed Heracles.

"I am not a child. No child has a knife like this, Prince Heracles."

"I agree; it's a beautiful knife. Now, go home."

"Try it."

"No."

"Then will you let me . . . ?"

Heracles shrugged his shoulders. "If I do, will you leave me and go home?"

Iolaus beamed with delight at his victory. To have pierced the Nemean lion would increase the value of his knife enormously; and to have helped Heracles would increase his own even more. A world of boys would gape and envy him. He stepped forward and his birthday knife flashed in the sun.

"Try to make the first cut in the throat," said Heracles, and wondered fleetingly what he would say if the boy succeeded. Iolaus knelt and, with a triumphant, admiring grin at Heracles, thrust his magnificent knife into the dead monster's neck.

"Never mind," murmured Heracles, uncomfortably relieved by Iolaus's suddenly dismayed face as the marvellous knife snapped off at the hilt. "I will give you another. No tears, now. You told me you weren't a child, Iolaus. . . ."

"I'm not crying," muttered Iolaus. "I—I've hurt my knee."

"Show me."

"It's nothing—"

"Then show me nothing."

Iolaus stood up. His knee was bleeding from a deep gash; he had been resting it on the dead monster's claw.

"I told you to go home," began Heracles, angry at being partly responsible for the boy's injury; then his eyes gleamed. He bent down, wrenched out one of the lion's huge claws and with it, pierced the iron-hard skin as easily as if it had been air.

"Without me," mumbled Iolaus, holding his broken knife, and dismally bleeding, "you would never have thought of it, Prince Heracles."

Heracles was about to answer when the crowd parted to make space for a messenger from the palace. This man, fastidious as his master, wrinkled his fine nose at the steam that rose from the perforated lion and averted his eyes from the withered entrails.

"Prince Heracles—?"

"I am Heracles."

"The king has decided—"

"Not the queen?"

"She too—she too, Heracles."

"Two minds with but a single thought? It's as well. One thought is food enough for two such minds."

The messenger compressed his lips as the crowd laughed and even the boy Iolaus folded his arms and frowned defiance on behalf of his hero.

"Perhaps it will be enough for you also, Prince Heracles. The Second Labour imposed upon you is—to destroy the Lernian Hydra."

The laughter died; a great sigh went up from the crowd, then a trembling seized them and they began to back away. In every heart dark terrors arose and the filthy stench of the creature seemed to invade the market place as the messenger pronounced its name. This evil creature lived in the swamps near Lerna, coming out only at night to lie across roads like a dark shadow from which no passing traveller emerged. Even the boy Iolaus shrank away from the man whose task it now was to go in search of the Hydra and drag it from the swamp. Already, in his mind's eye, he saw Heracles screaming in the Hydra's coils—and, try as he might, he could not put the sight out of his mind as it fascinated him horribly. . . .

Heracles alone seemed unmoved; he continued with his task of flaying the lion and did not give the messenger even the trifling triumph of raising his head and showing a face that had gone as pale as death.

"The Hydra," repeated the messenger. "The nine-headed

monster of the swamp. Kill it, Heracles; kill it, kill it!" His voice had risen to a gleeful screech; then he flushed and departed hastily. . . .

Moonshine drenched the market place of Mycenae and turned the piled-up guts of the perforated lion into a mound of silver that seemed to have been left over from making the beaten skin. Heracles stood up; someone was watching him.

"Who's there?"

A figure emerged from the shadow of an empty stall. It was Iolaus, his knee preposterously bandaged.

"What do you want now, child?"

Iolaus looked surprised, as if he'd not expected such a question.

"What are you going to do with the lion skin, Prince Heracles?"

"I don't know. . . ."

"Can I have it?"

"No."

"If it hadn't been for me, it would still be full of lion."

"And if it hadn't been for me, Iolaus, it might, one day, have been full of you."

"All right, then. You keep it."

"Many thanks."

"Wear it, Prince Heracles. Wear it like a cloak with the head for a helmet. Then all the world will know what you've done and what a great hero you are."

"Is that what you'd do, Iolaus?"

"Naturally."

"If I wear it, will you do something for me?"

"Be proud to, Prince Heracles."

"Go home."

"Not possible."

"Why not?"

"Why, I'm coming with you—to Lerna—to fight the Hydra."

Heracles stared at the boy in amazement; but Iolaus was in earnest, and nothing Heracles could say shook his resolve. He had told his parents that he was to be the companion of Prince Heracles; he had told his friends; he had told, it seemed, half of Mycenae. To go back now would not be possible. He would have to hang himself to escape the shame of it. Besides, he had helped

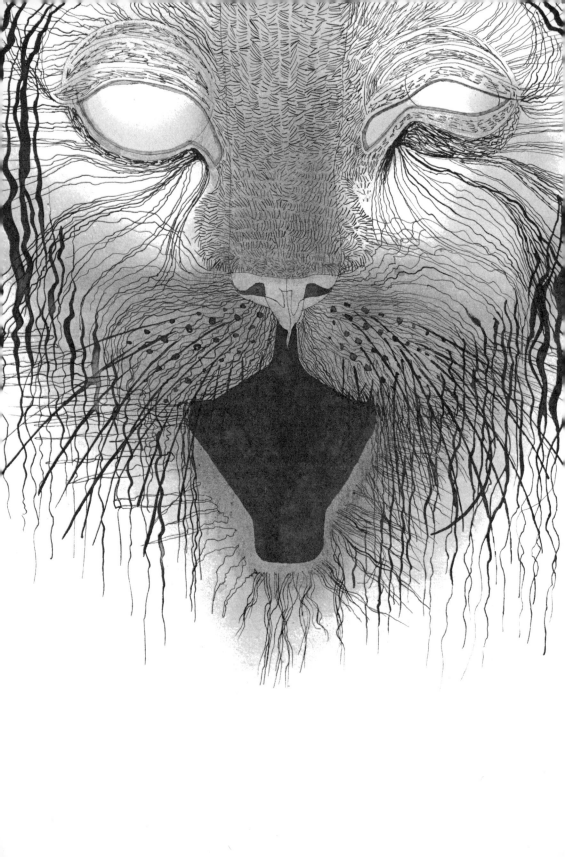

Heracles once, and it was very likely he'd be useful again. Surely Heracles could see the justice of this?

All this came out of Iolaus with great eloquence and earnestness. Nothing seemed to deter the boy, and when his hero picked up the lion skin and began to leave the market place, he followed, still arguing.

"You are taller than I am, Prince Heracles, so you can walk much faster. But I'll follow even though you leave me a mile behind. Maybe robbers will catch me and murder me? Think of that, Prince Heracles. People will say you left me to be killed; and no one will think well of you for that. Besides, I've still a bad knee, got, I may say, in helping you. I fancy that will make it sound worse. But if that's what you want, stride on ahead, Prince Heracles, and I'll hobble after till the wolves get me. . . ."

Heracles halted and waited for the boy to catch up with him. He scowled; but felt, at the same time, a most unwilling affection for him. Iolaus limped to just beyond an arm's reach of his hero.

"Iolaus, of all the Labours King Eurystheus could devise, *you* are the hardest to bear with."

Iolaus did not look in the least offended; he accepted the fact that he was a nuisance as if it was nothing original to him.

"Why are you so anxious to be rid of me, Prince Heracles? Are you frightened the madness will come over you again and you'll kill me as they say you killed your own children? Yes; I know all about that and am not at all afraid. So there can be no call for you to be. And if it's my father and mother that's troubling you—for everyone says you're very particular about such things—then I give you my solemn word and I'll swear by the River Styx, if you like, that their last words to me were that whatever becomes of me will be by the will of the gods and my own fault; mostly my own fault. No blame on you at all. . . ."

Heracles gazed at Iolaus, half-smiling, half-inclined to weep; his heart thundered as if it would break open his chest. He was filled with terror at this child who dared to speak of his hideous, loathsome guilt as innocently as if it formed a bond between them instead of an abyss that separated him from the rest of mankind. His eyes filled with tears and through them he saw Iolaus, multiplied into a host of boys, standing just beyond an arm's reach away.

Iolaus, briefly silent, watched Heracles hopefully and a shade uneasily; plainly the boy was wondering what further arguments he could bring in support of his case. He opened his mouth as if for a further stretch of eloquence when Heracles lifted his hand as if to ward it off; then Heracles smiled and put on the lion skin in silent acknowledgement of Iolaus's victory.

Though privately he thought he looked ridiculous, he was nevertheless deeply moved to see the open admiration and delight in Iolaus's face. It was no little thing to Heracles to be the hero of the young, to be great in eyes before they'd grown the worldly cataracts of envy, failure and spite. . . .

Together they left Mycenae and travelled southward through the night—a curious pair under the moon: the tall, magnificent man wearing a lion's skin so that, in certain tricks of light and shade, he looked like the lion itself, dancing upright to the will of the limping boy whose huge bandage kept coming undone until it was lost altogether—and with it, the limp.

They rested for the latter end of the night by the northern banks of the River Inachus; then, soon after dawn, they crossed the river by a ford and continued southward towards Lerna.

They passed between Argos and Tiryns, meeting with village children who stared at them in awe—until bolder spirits among them darted close to tug at the lion's empty tail. This angered Iolaus and irritated Heracles, who blamed Iolaus for bringing it upon him with his insistence on wearing the skin. But Iolaus looked so dejected by the reproach that Heracles relented and offered to let the boy carry his wild olive club. Iolaus flushed with pride. He took the rough wood as if it was the world's sceptre and set off once more with the enormous weapon on his shoulder.

"Prince Heracles—"

"Yes, Iolaus?"

"It's not that I'm not tremendously honoured to be carrying your club—which, after all, is famous everywhere; but—"

"But what?"

"It's not that I'm not strong enough. Please don't imagine that. It's the weather, Prince Heracles. The air seems to have grown so warm and heavy. . . ."

Heracles paused and glanced up to the noonday sky; it was clear and bright. He stared curiously at Iolaus, and relieved him of his burden.

"Will you carry my quiver of arrows, Iolaus?"

"The arrows made by the gods?"

"So I was told, Iolaus."

Iolaus beamed, slung the quiver across his back and marched briskly in Heracles's wake. But in a little while, the quiver too seemed to gain mysterious weight, and threatened to rub a hole in the boy's shoulder. Dismally he loitered after the tall, striding figure whose shadow, short under the high sun, bounded and snapped at his feet like the ghost of the lion pursuing its dancing skin. "Would to the gods it would catch him and hold him back!" thought Iolaus, who was reluctant to complain again and hoped vainly that Heracles would notice his distress of his own accord.

The landscape had begun to descend towards wide valleys where plane trees grew abundantly—in groves, copses and curious woods that resembled old green cities whose crowding pillars had caught a stone-fever and come out in blotches and spots. . . .

The green was amazingly brilliant—on account of the moisture always in the ground. This moisture ceaselessly forced its way up from certain secret streams that ran underneath the earth's skin like silver veins, rupturing here and there into springs that fed wells and small, uncanny rivers that wound among the rich grass as if looking for something. . . .

Heracles's pace never slackened, consequently the distance between him and his unhappy arrow-bearer increased. At times Iolaus was forced to break into a heavy, painful run to keep Heracles in sight; on these occasions Heracles would pause and stare back at the boy with an odd expression in his eyes.

An uneasiness began to creep round the boy's heart and he could not keep from wondering what look had been in Heracles's grey eyes when he'd gazed on his sons for the last time. . . . He found himself unable to put this disturbing thought out of his mind; his pace grew even slower and there were moments when Heracles disappeared from sight, in a fold of ground or beyond a clump of trees. On one such occasion, Heracles lay in wait for him, crouching in a dip of land; then leaped up, lion's head over his face and roaring ferociously. Iolaus cried out in terror at the suddenness of it; and despite Heracles's laughing apologies and earnest promises never to do such a thing again, the boy's face remained desperately pale.

"Let's rest awhile," proposed Heracles.

They seated themselves, but the ground was unpleasantly wet and there was a sickly, sweetish smell in the air that gave Iolaus a headache. His immense powers of conversation seemed to have deserted him, else they were turned inward as he argued himself in and out of a thousand shadowy fears.

Heracles stood up and offered the boy his hand. Iolaus took it, but could not repress a slight shudder. They walked slowly now, side by side, and Heracles questioned Iolaus about his home, his ambitions and his best possessions. Iolaus answered sullenly, with a trudge in his voice . . . so Heracles fell to telling him of his own childhood, of the grand palace at Thebes and the strangled serpents; then he found himself drifting on about his battle with the God of Death on the road to Aornum and the rescue of Alcestis. He'd always longed to talk about it, then he remembered how he'd been prevented before. His eyes clouded, his lips tightened and a furrow deepened in his brow. Iolaus peered at him as if trying to penetrate the meaning of this new expression.

Neither of them spoke of the Hydra, yet they could not have been far from its lair. The very path they trod, devoid of grass, might have been a passing track of the creature's: its slime was poisonous, it killed where it crept. If the evil thing was in their thoughts, it stayed as silent and deep as in the Lernian swamp.

Presently they came to a rough wooden house, built on piles sunk into the soft ground.

"Shall we go in, Iolaus?"

The boy looked down. An inexplicable feeling of depression and shame overwhelmed him. He muttered something inaudible.

"Then I will go in," said Heracles. "For we need a torch. It will be dark when we reach the swamp."

He left Iolaus and the boy waited, his thoughts twisting and turning in his head. He took off the heavy quiver and withdrew an arrow. He stared at it, thinking of legendary bowmen and other heroes. He remembered an evening long ago when he'd been allowed to stay up late because a bald old storyteller had come to his father's house for a night's lodging in exchange for a tale by the fire. "Listen well, Iolaus," his father had said; "and learn how splendid the world once was." The old man had bleated of gods and heroes, of Meleager and Atalanta and fierce Peleus. He'd glorified them, and yet, when all was said and done, they'd been no more than huge, clumsy murderers.

Now he despised the storyteller for his lies, and he despised himself for his childish hero-worshipping of the worst murderer of all: Heracles the child killer. He fingered the arrow's sharp bronze point; he could do the world a favour and kill Heracles with it. . . .

"Carry this, Iolaus, and I'll take the quiver."

Heracles stood behind him holding out a newly kindled torch. Iolaus took it and somehow the smell of the burning pitch seemed to subdue the worst of his fears.

By now the sun had dropped down and stood briefly behind a wall of trees from where it shot its last bright spears and arrows; but this archery soon ceased; the sky darkened, shadows closed up the gaps in the trees and Iolaus's torch was left alone to resist the advancing night.

He carried it as high as the thickening vegetation would allow; but despite great care, it kept catching against branches and disgorging sudden showers of flaring pitch that hissed to extinction in the shining ground. These abrupt explosions of light momentarily extended the view and revealed that the landscape had substantially changed its nature; the plane trees had given way to pale, sinewy willows rooted in mud; clumps of reeds and marsh grass sprang into sight, then passed back into darkness, lingering only where their tips had been ignited by stray droppings from the torch: they flared and smouldered like marigolds in hell. The ground underfoot had become loose and clutched at the feet; the sickly, sweetish smell that had been in the air since mid-afternoon had increased markedly and was now overpoweringly strong.

Presently a most curious and uncanny effect was seen: as the torch penetrated further and further into the deteriorating region, a faint image or echo of it appeared, sometimes ahead and sometimes to one side. At times even vague outlines of Heracles and Iolaus, like gossamer shadows, were visible beside it. This puzzling effect seemed to be produced by a dense, steamy mist that hung above certain fingers and patches of ground and reflected the passing light. Yet as the mist was permeable, this explanation did not altogether satisfy.

Onward movement now became hazardous; the firm places had been steadily diminishing until, quite suddenly, they came to an end. Heracles and Iolaus halted. Before them stretched a wide area—a lake—of gently moving slime; upon this smooth surface, dimly visible in the cloying mist, stood a tall figure and a shorter one, holding aloft a flaming torch. The remoteness and silence of the vision was very striking; in several places about the feet of the phantom images, soft, slow bubbles rose up and burst, discharging the heavy sweetish smell that was a characteristic of the entire region.

"Fire," whispered Heracles. "Give me fire." The heavy secrecy of the place oppressed all sound, so that even the whisper intruded sharply.

The torch was thrust towards him, dangerously close to his eyes. Through the veils of flame he saw Iolaus's face; he looked aside and touched the fire with an arrow head till the pitch ran over the bronze and the arrow was aflame. Then he sent it flaring into the misty swamp to meet its swift reflection and vanish with a sudden hiss. Three more burning arrows followed, arching over the quiet slime; and multiplied reflections, racing across the surface and flying out of the curtained air, turned the night into an angry design of loosely threading fire. Then all rushed to extinction—the threads of fire, the reflected torchlight and the shadowy figures together. It was as if the arrows of Heracles had extinguished a dream.

The darkened mist swirled; heads came through it—flat, gleaming heads sistering each other on rocking necks. Twisting deeply together, these necks united in a wider vessel in which they throbbed like swollen veins. . . . It was the Hydra; silently it had kept pace behind the mist, casting back the phantom reflections from its glass-smooth skin.

"Iolaus," breathed Heracles, "set the trees afire. . . ."

Iolaus hesitated, then with a last look at Heracles and the nine heads rocking out of the mist, fled with his torch streaming high. As he ran, tearing the brand through invisible obstructions, storms of sparks rushed down, stinging his cheeks and arms; he heard twigs and branches begin to spit and crackle. The night trembled into a sullen redness, throwing into striking relief the shapes made by smoke pouring down through the interstices of the flaring trees. Such shapes, deformed and bulkily crimson, looked like the hidden thoughts of the air itself to which the smoke had given tell-tale substance.

Suddenly, over and above the spiteful clamour of the fire,

Iolaus heard a violent crashing noise; but terror prevented him looking back. He fancied he heard a cry, but even then he ran on, driven by an overmastering feeling of disgust.

"Iolaus!"

The voice was wild and shaking. The boy hesitated; then, against all his pressing instincts, he turned.

The Hydra had come out of the swamp. He saw it between the trees, huge and shining in the irregular firelight. Its extremities, numerous and flexible as its nest of necks, were twined about Heracles who seemed unable to move. Its nine heads jostled his face, which was turned towards Iolaus with a look of such mortal anguish that the boy forgot the last of his fears of Heracles.

An immense distress and pity seized him as he watched the world's great hero being slowly murdered by the stench and filth of the Hydra. Why was Heracles so still? Why were his great arms hanging limply as if he was already dead? Bewildered, Iolaus blundered towards the engulfing Hydra, crying out, "Fight back! For pity's sake, fight back!"

Heracles saw him. "Go . . . go . . ." he wept; then other heads came between him and Iolaus. The heads Heracles saw on the Hydra's necks were the heads of the children he'd slaughtered in the courtyard at Thebes. They smiled at him, jostled close for kisses. . . . Why were they so cold?

Madness in reverse had taken hold of him; he saw children where there were snakes. Such was the power of the Hydra that it caused each man to fight against himself—and then consumed him in forgetful slime. This was the testing time of Heracles, facing the vengeance of his deepest dreads. He felt his chest being squeezed and squeezed; his lungs were choked with evil smells; and his beloved sons opened their rosy mouths to give him nipping bites with teeth as bright as pearls.

"Strike at it! Strike at it!" cried Iolaus.

Heracles shuddered; he raised his arm—but not the one that held his club—and caressed the eager cheeks and stroked the obstinately tangled heads.

"Strike them off!" screamed Iolaus.

The flames leaped and crackled; branches crashed—and eyes like clustering stars rocked and danced in the air.

"The madness," groaned Heracles. "*This* is the madness!"

He lifted the hand that held his club, and gave a cry as if

begging forgiveness; then he struck with all his might at the beloved heads. Whole trees roared into fire, holding up their branches as if to ward off the intense heat. Again and again Heracles struck—and the heads fell like rotten fruit with black blood gushing from the ruptured necks.

Iolaus shouted out in triumph—then his voice died. The black blood bubbled and crusted even as it flowed; and out of the crust rose new heads—two on every neck, then two again as each of these new born heads fell to Heracles's club. A hundred Hydras sprouted from the one; a teeming multitude of snakes waved about Heracles, like the stamens of some huge, grey flower. . . .

"Burn out the necks! Use the torch, Iolaus! The necks—sear them!"

Iolaus crept close; a head fell, cold and wet against his foot. He leaped back in horror—but then advanced again, holding out the torch till it found the blinded neck. He touched it with the dripping pitch; it hissed and shrank, then dropped like a length of dirty rope.

"The necks—the necks!" panted Heracles. So Iolaus found them; the dark blood boiled and steamed, the flesh shrivelled and the dead necks fell in loose disarray. Little by little the crowding heads diminished—like a multitude departing—as the club of Heracles thrashed among them and Iolaus's fire scalded the stumps. Vague heaps of them glimmered on the ground, like a windfall from an eerie tree . . . but all the while there was one head that did not fall: the head that contained the Hydra's brain. In vain Heracles battered at it, but it continued to lunge and dance and while it lived, the grip about Heracles grew tighter and tighter. . . .

Suddenly he felt a terrible pain in his foot. He glanced down. A crab had crawled from the swamp and had seized hold of his heel. Secure in its shell that must have seemed a mighty fortress, it had crawled to the aid of its monstrous companion from the slime: a scavenging Iolaus to its Heracles foul as sin.

He shouted in anger at the mockery and stamped the crab to fragments. Then he looked up. The Hydra's last head was close to his own. No maddened illusion now, no false image, but the flat, bland countenance of poison itself. Heracles saw himself deformed in its cold eyes. He saw appalling knowledge in its slow, gaping smile, knowledge of his darkest self—and of dark-

ness everywhere. Knowledge without wisdom, without pity, without light.

"My sword, Iolaus! Give me my sword—"

The Hydra's jaws widened. Heracles, with the precision of extreme fear, saw venom bubbling in its throat, saw its divided tongue flicker and plunge. . . .

"Quickly! The sword!"

He dropped his club and stretched out his hand. He felt the sword—the Hydra's eyes grew deep and deeper; the double image of Heracles seemed to whirl away into their depths—then the sword flashed. The head fell and the Lernian Hydra was dead.

Hastily, and with eyes averted, Heracles and Iolaus buried the Hydra's head under a stone. This done, Heracles dipped a pair of arrows into the black blood that was steadily soaking into the ground. These arrows he marked with notches; the smallest scratch from them would procure certain death. They were to be used only in the last extremity. Lastly, Heracles dragged the huge, flabby corpse of the Hydra back to the swamp where he and Iolaus watched it sink under the slow folds of slime from which it had emerged. By way of an ironic tribute, Heracles cast the pieces of the broken crab onto the mirror-smooth surface of the swamp—to mark the place where the Hydra lay. For a few moments they floated, glinting like tattered stars; then they sank and the swamp forgot them.

Iolaus felt Heracles's hand on his shoulder. He glanced up into his hero's face, which was ruddy and shining in the firelight. How was it possible that he'd ever feared this man?

"Come, Iolaus."

Iolaus nodded; and then, taking with them two of the severed heads as evidence of what had been done, he and Heracles made their way among the glowing trees like two weary souls finding their way out of hell.

13 • Cleanliness is Next to Godliness

Eurystheus, King of Mycenae, had a friend. Not to put too fine a point upon it, this friend smelled; indeed, he stank, and though he lived many miles to the west, in Elis, there were times when the wind was right—or wrong—when Eurystheus wrinkled his sensitive nose and murmured: "Ah! Augeias. . . ."

Strange, that a pair so cultured and fastidious as Eurystheus and his queen should have such a friend as filthy Augeias. But there were reasons. Augeias was a king—which accounted for some of them; and Augeias was immensely rich—which accounted for the rest. Though the King and Queen of Mycenae would have shrunk from a smelly, verminous beggar—might even have had him scourged from the kingdom—a smelly, verminous rich man was another kettle of stinking fish altogether. Whereas the beggar was dirty because he couldn't help it, the rich man must have had his reasons. There must have been something in it; and even if it was only a bad smell, it was a bad smell chosen by a personage rich and powerful enough to have taken his pick.

Augeias was large and fat, with a loose smile on his lips and a hunted look in his small eyes—as if there was, somewhere inside, a thinner, cleaner Augeias, constantly criticising him.

This King of Elis was the wretched victim of a timid nature and extraordinary good luck. Neither famine nor pestilence ever touched his lands, and twelve silver white bulls, that had appeared from nowhere, guarded his immense herds against marauding wild beasts. It was uncanny how everything conspired to enrich him—and he was frightened by it. His natural timidity kept whispering that he was riding for a fall; there were times, even, when he actually longed for disaster to strike, just to have it over and done with and no longer hanging over his too-fortunate head.

This apprehension had the effect of freezing his will so that, in time, he reached the pitiable state of being unable to make even the smallest decision for fear of its bringing about the calamity he dreaded. All he could do was to sit, in mounting confusion and filth, watching his wealth increase with a grin of terrified delight.

Horses and cattle had been the foundation of his riches; his huge stables, with their marble stalls and porcelain troughs, had been a wonder of the world. The mosaic floor was said to have been designed by Apollo himself; but many years had passed since that floor had been seen, and even the stables themselves had sunk under a disagreeable obscurity. No one wanted anything to do with them; responsibility was shifted from servant to servant with a fluent ease that altogether baffled Augeias. He lost his temper frequently, but was totally unable to make up his mind. Consequently the stables had not been cleaned. He had been putting off this trifling decision from day to day for the past thirty years. Nowadays when men spoke of Mount Elis, they did not mean any lofty eminence clothed in trees and crowned with sun-gilded rock; they meant the terraced range of dung under which the stables of Augeias had long since vanished and over which there always hung a thundercloud of flies. Sometimes this cloud would lift as bulging mares or cows would toil across the steamy skyline, pause and add to the awful landscape. Then the cloud would reassemble with a buzzing that filled the air in and about the palace.

Somewhere in the palace Augeias had a wife and several sons; but as they were as neglected and filthy as everything else, he would never be quite sure whether they or his servants had answered him back. It was only strangers he could be sure of—and then all the consciousness of his Royal state came upon him, in case he should be taken for someone too poor to keep his house in order.

"My dabe is Heracles," said the tall young man in the lion's skin who stood before him and spoke as if he had a severe cold or else his nostrils were plugged. . . .

"Cousin of my good friend Eurystheus?"

"By order of the gods I serve Eurystheus," answered Heracles, not proud to claim the relationship.

"Nevertheless, same family," said Augeias, hopelessly scratching himself. "Breeding shows. Never be put off by clothes or appearances. High family can be seen directly. You'd be surprised, people sometimes wonder about me; but men of family, I've noticed, always know one another."

"Oh, yes," murmured Heracles, staring up at the abominable king on his grimy throne. Augeias fidgeted, obscurely sensing criticism.

"I could buy and sell you ten times over, Heracles," he said, pursuing a private line of thought.

"Ah, but could you buy be and keep be?" said Heracles humorously; he could not find it in his heart to dislike this gross, pathetic man.

"Have you a cold, Heracles?" asked Augeias, irritably. The smallest suggestion of wit annoyed him. Eurystheus had often been witty at his expense; but Eurystheus was a king, after all. . . . "I won't have diseased men here. I am very particular about health, Heracles. I consider sickness as something unclean. And next to sickness I abhor insolence. For a servant of Eurystheus, Heracles, you give yourself too many airs."

"Ah, but they're nothing beside yours, King Augeias," said Heracles, removing his plugs and wrinkling his nose. He made a mental note to repeat this witticism to young Iolaus, who was waiting in the palace yard.

Augeias gnawed his fingernails and was unable to make up his mind whether he'd been flattered or insulted. Heracles spoke again: "I have come, King Augeais, to clean out your stables."

For a moment Augeias failed to take in what Heracles had said. Then his fat lips wobbled; his eyes disappeared in swamps of flesh; and he heaved with laughter. At last he had seen a joke.

"The Labours of Heracles! I've heard . . . oh, yes! Great tasks! But one must pay for arrogance! So now it's Heracles in the—ha-ha!—in the dung! King of the dunghill!"

As Augeias shook with grubby merriment, Heracles's eyes glittered with anger. He recalled the reason for his Labours; the dark immensity of his crime. The task now set him seemed to belittle, not him, but what he had done. He raged inwardly as he remembered his gigantic grief. Was it now to be set on a level with a lifetime's heaving filth?

"All your days, Heracles!" puffed Augeias, breaking wind in his happy excitement. "In the dung! For I promise you, my cattle will undo each night what you've laboured over each day! What a life, Heracles, stretches before you!"

"A day, Augeias!" shouted Heracles, his eyes full of angry tears. "That's all you'll have from me! A single day of mine to clear up your lifetime's filth! I'll do it by nightfall, Augeias. I swear it by my father's name."

But Augeias, in the full flood of his triumphant mirth, was not to be deflected. He was absolutely delighted he'd stung Heracles into making so rash a boast; he regarded it as a moral victory.

"Ha-ha! Which father, Heracles? I've heard there is some doubt!"

"Zeus!" roared Heracles, beside himself with a fury he was already regretting but was unable to control. When he'd made the oath he had, in fact, meant Amphitryon, his mother's husband, whose name, after all, would have been somewhat less binding than Zeus's. But now it was too late. Augeias was grinning incredulously. His victory had suddenly assumed divine proportions.

"Witnesses!" cried Augeias. "Witnesses to the oath of Heracles! Who are you?" This last to an unappetising-looking youth with a beard like a spider's 'prentice work.

"Phyleus, father—"

"Ah, my first-born. Well, well; never mind. Just witness the oath Heracles here has taken. Clear out your mind of rubbish and just remember this. It's all I ask. Heracles has sworn by Zeus to clean the stables by nightfall."

The youth looked dully at the scene, then nodded; the oath was confirmed and Heracles was committed to clear away in one day what had taken thirty neglectful years to accumulate.

"Please don't think I'm complaining, Prince Heracles—or even suggesting that you lost your temper, but I think you were a bit hasty with the king."

Iolaus stared up and up until he could just make out the long, rambling summit of the terraced mountain with its ominous thundercloud of flies. Foothills had long since overflowed the stable walls and ambled on across the nearby fields. Steam rose from the whole region, as if it was volcanic; and the unending procession of fatted cattle moving through the wispy vapours and mounting laboriously upward suggested some strange and godless allegory of vanity and ambition.

"Also it's very degrading," went on Iolaus, who had come to regard himself as the admiring conscience of Heracles. "After all, you are the greatest hero in the world: the son of Zeus and all that. I don't mind it at all for myself, you understand; but it seems to me that—"

"—Why should it be more degrading to clean up filth than to make it?" interrupted Heracles irritably. The task appalled him no less than it did Iolaus; the reeking air offended him just as much; to be reproached for his rashness was no help at all.

"The point is well taken," said Iolaus, who'd picked up the expression from his father. "And if I might make a suggestion, Prince Heracles, the sooner we make a beginning, the sooner we'll make an end."

Heracles, leaning against a portion of the wall that had somehow escaped the attention of the cattle, scowled. He looked about him, but did not seem inclined to take up Iolaus's suggestion.

"There are times, child, when a little thought might save a mountain of labour."

Iolaus shrugged his shoulders and joined the world's hero at the wall, leaning in the same attitude and scowling with the same appearance of concentration. Heracles looked at him suspiciously.

"What are you doing, Iolaus?"

"Thinking."

Heracles compressed his lips. "Do you see the baskets King Augeias has provided?"

Iolaus nodded.

"How long would it take you to carry one to the river?"

"Empty?"

"Filled, Iolaus."

The boy sighed, and gazed northward across the fouled landscape to where a narrow river ran, with furtive eagerness, towards the distant sea. There was another river—a tributary of some larger stream—that ran a sluggish course some way further to the south. Iolaus took it that Heracles meant the swifter and nearer of the two streams.

"Not long, Prince Heracles."

"Then make a beginning, Iolaus, and I'll measure the time."

Iolaus opened his mouth as if to say something. Heracles looked at him inquiringly; and Iolaus changed his mind. He sighed again and picked up a basket.

"Where's the spade, Prince Heracles?"

"Hands were made before spades, Iolaus."

Iolaus smiled feebly, looked up at the thundercloud-capped heights of the gruesome Mount Elis, then he looked down at his own small hands. Finally he looked at Heracles, who had not stirred from the wall and was nodding encouragingly.

"They say many hands make light work, Prince Heracles."

"So they do, Iolaus. Use both."

So Iolaus, with frequent glances at straight-faced Heracles, filled the basket and set off towards the river—a tiny figure pitted against the mountain of confusion and filth. But it seemed that Heracles had intended, not the nearer stream, but the other, more sluggish one. He shouted and pointed to a place where rocks were already causing a silting of the river bed. Wearily Iolaus changed direction, discharged his burden where he'd been bidden, and returned.

"Again, Iolaus."

"Meaning no offence, Prince Heracles; but there *is* a second basket. . . ."

"Taking no offence, Iolaus—I don't think you could manage both. But, by all means, try."

Iolaus stared hard at his hero, searching his lips and eyes for the glimmer of a smile. But Heracles's face remained profoundly innocent of mockery; so Iolaus filled the basket again and plodded off to the river, muttering in his heart all manner of mutinies and harsh rebukes to heroes brooding under the morning sun. The bitterest blow of all was when he observed that Heracles had a spade.

"I see spades have been made at last," said Iolaus with biting irony. Heracles nodded affably, but made no move to part with it.

"I helped him skin the Nemean Lion," mumbled Iolaus to himself. "I helped him slay the Lernian Hydra. He might at least help me to clean the Augeian Stables."

Nevertheless he continued to toil away at the ignominious task to which hero-worshipping had brought him. Vainly he tried to call up in his mind all the golden images he'd had of Heracles in earlier days; then, when this failed, he wondered why he was submitting to his present degradation. After all, it was Heracles who'd sinned and so had been set the Labours. He, Iolaus, was as pure as a newborn lamb. If he had any sense at all he'd leave Elis here and now. He'd go back to Mycenae and spread the bitter news that Heracles, as a hero, left a good deal to be desired.

Yet Iolaus did not return to Mycenae. He had a certain streak of obstinacy in his nature that prevented him admitting to any error of judgement. When he admired, he continued to admire; when he loved, he continued to love. He preferred to make excuses for others than for himself. So, Heracles had his faults. . . .

Then, shortly before noon, Iolaus saw that Heracles had stirred himself. He was setting to work. At once all Iolaus's doubts and reproaches vanished. A great joy filled him. Forgotten was the vile nature of the Labour; all that mattered was that Heracles was undertaking it. Amazed, Iolaus saw that a great hole had been breached in the stable wall. Such an aperture through the burly stone would have taken a dozen strong men a full day to achieve . . . well, maybe half a day; Iolaus in his delight was given to exaggeration. Next, he saw Heracles in the fields. He was digging; and as if for the first time the boy had an inkling of his hero's strength. He had seen Heracles wrestle with the Hydra, but now he saw him wrestling with the size of the land itself. There were many men broader in the shoulder than Heracles, thicker in the arm and calf; but there never was a man who had quite that perfection of strength so that power and grace were united, each serving the other without the smallest wastage.

The spoiled earth flew and the land seemed to divide in Heracles's wake. By mid-afternoon there was a deep channel from the breached wall almost reaching a bend in the fast-running stream. Then, with formidable speed, Heracles set about changing the course of the second river. Already swollen and sluggishly flooding its banks on account of Iolaus's labours, this stream—a remote tributary of the River Alpheus—blundered down a second channel to join its waters with the swifter running Menius at a point above the vulnerable bend. For a moment the double flow leaped; it foamed and struggled at its banks like some silver prisoner awakening to an intolerable constriction.

Furiously it flung itself against the bend, as if frantic for a straighter course. The pressed earth bulged ominously towards the empty channel. Again and again Heracles struck with his spade until at last, with a violent commotion, the aneurism ruptured: the river tumbled through its new outlet and rushed on towards the stable wall.

It met it with a thunderous eruption; halted briefly, rising and spreading until the immense weight of water confirmed the breach in the stone. Then, slowly at first, but with increasing ease, it pierced the breach and the river moved onward through the buried stables.

Still holding his basket, Iolaus watched with amazement and awe till, catching sight of Heracles standing with folded arms, he did likewise and stared up at Mount Elis.

At first only the thundercloud of flies showed signs of unnatural agitation. It is the tiniest creatures in nature that first observe those minute motions, hidden from larger eyes, that are the advanced patrols of the oncoming army of calamity. The cloud rose, shivered, spread into its million buzzing particles, then condensed again into curious shadow-figures—like some hastily-scrawled message of dismay. Certain mares and cows, stumbling across the upper terraces, began whinnying and lowing uneasily; a silver-white bull that had stood like a marble monarch sombrely watching his loaded queens, bellowed with alarm and plunged down the slopes. The mountain had begun to move.

Its abominable foundations having been undermined by the forcing waters, the whole huge structure began to curtsey to the sky. Rifts appeared, closed up only to give way to deeper openings and fallings-in. The skyline sank; the mountain shuddered down to a hill. Tops of walls, capitals of pillars, portions of ribbed roofs long since hidden, appeared like a vast bony structure poking through to the air.

The sight was weird and grand beyond all expectation; nor was this all. The river's energies continued; a tide of dung—a moving highway—surged out of the stables as the waters made their own broad course towards the relief of sea. The landscape seemed to stand aside in bewilderment: horses and cattle huddled in panic-stricken groups; but the indomitable cloud of flies, buzzing philosophically, followed the moving road to see where the tale would end.

Little by little they dwindled away until they were no more than a tiny smudge against the western sky. The sun came down as if to burn them up and flooded the landscape with a brand-new evening light. Mount Elis had gone, and the river flowed silver through the resurrected stables of Augeias.

Heracles turned his face to catch the last fires of the setting sun. "Father Zeus," he smiled. "See: I did not take your name in vain."

The Augeian Stables, all marble and pale blue porcelain, gleamed under the next day's sky. Timorously the cattle approached, gazing in wonderment at the pillared paradise which, perhaps, their long-dead sires and dams had told them of, and which had been lost under the mountains of slime. So there really had been a stable after all. . . .

Ceaselessly the diverted river ran through the well-constructed gullies and endlessly washed the floor. The only filthy object in the whole building was King Augeias himself; the Labour of Heracles had not included him.

A vague sense of loss oppressed the shabby, verminous monarch. There was more sky about than ever he remembered; and the air smelled hard and sharp and went through his head like a knife. He sat on a carved coping-stone and helplessly dabbled his feet in the chuckling water till a general pinkness appeared that quite fascinated him.

The floor—the glorious mosaic floor—stretched out before him, shining under veils and veils of the stream. He peered at it and blinked away some tears. It was very beautiful; it depicted, in addition to miraculous cattle, Augeias himself; but a younger, slender Augeias in the first blush of royalty and the pride of youth. He'd quite forgotten about it. Dimly he recognised himself and wondered uncomfortably whether the floor had been covered up by neglect or design. Slowly he took off his robes, lowered himself from the stone and began, compulsively, to wash and wash and wash. . . .

14 • A Journey into Hell

Mycenae was full of strangers; mothers with their children, calling vainly after husbands who'd wandered off on their own to peer at buildings, scorning the talkative guide.

"And here," said the guide, having shepherded his flock to the market place, "is where great Heracles skinned the Nemean Lion. Purses of blood-stained sand may be bought from the stalls. . . ."

At once children began to pester to buy mementoes and an old man, who'd joined the procession, smiled wryly and shook his bald head. He himself presented heroes complete and in the brightest colours, and got no more for his pains than a night's lodging. How much more profitable it was to trade in mementoes than in memories. What a world wherein a pinch of dirty sand weighed more in the balance than a golden dream!

"And here is the very post where great Heracles tethered the fearful Bull of Crete," droned the guide; and the storyteller took his place in the queue to examine the scorching of the wood from the monster's breath. He touched it—and the guide warned him sharply against damaging the relic. He took the old man by the arm and led him firmly to where four hoofprints, carved in stone, had been let into the sandy ground. They were impossibly far apart.

"The Boar of Erymanthus," said the guide. "The fifth of great Heracles's Labours."

"Was it not the fourth?" said the storyteller wearily. "Was it not after he cleaned the Stables of Augeias?"

"Old man," said the guide with a touch of irritation, "we have seen these things and you have not. Listen and don't presume to teach."

Humbly the storyteller bowed his head. Who was he to oppose

an eye-witness? He shuffled on in the wake of the viewing party. As he peered and listened, his thoughts drifted back to his visit to the palace at Argos when he'd seen Atalanta's cloak and sandals, her quiver of arrows and the broken threads of her races. He remembered the long golden hair he'd treasured—and then let vanish away on the evening air. He could have sold that hair, he reflected with a melancholy smile. . . .

"Here, old man—take it and say nothing," said the guide quietly; he handed the storyteller several splinters of scorched wood. "You look as though memories mean a great deal to you. Take these mementoes of great Heracles's Labours . . . and may they bring you pleasant dreams."

Gratefully the old man tucked the splinters in his wallet; but then, once outside Mycenae, he took them out and dropped them in the sand.

"The world I build," he mumbled with some arrogance, "wants no such foundations!"

He glanced back at the city, fiery under the setting sun. He marked the palace of the king where, in his mind's eye, he saw Eurystheus and his queen, like a pair of improbable spiders, waiting the return of a Heracles even more improbable than they.

"But I'll change you," murmured the storyteller, turning his back on the city, "into something better than burnt wood, stone hoofprints and dirty sand. My Heracles will be almost a god. . . ."

"He has aged, you know. He has thickened. His step is heavier; and the arrogance has gone. That pleases me. The fires have gone out of his eyes."

The King of Mycenae smiled thoughtfully as he lay back on the couch in his underground bronze jar. He peered up to where he could just see his queen's pale forehead and vague hair circling the rim like a cumbersome moth. Round and round she went, casting in her meed of spite and contempt like the ingredients of a venomous stew. Such was the vigil of Eurystheus and his wife whenever Heracles returned to Mycenae to learn what his next Labour was to be.

For eight years he had served them, journeying at their bidding into kingdoms out of mind. Wherever the winds blew blackest and the nights were filled with poison, he pursued, wrestled with and overcame all the weird monsters dredged up from Eurystheus's fastidious brain.

"His time is running out. Soon he will have escaped us. He will go free in the world; maybe even to turn on you. Think of that. . . ." The queen's voice came down into the huge metallic chamber, filling it with whispering echoes and sharpening Eurystheus's thoughts. Ten Labours had been accomplished; only two more remained. . . .

"Think, Eurystheus. . . ."

The queen's voice had coarsened, even as she had herself. Her hair was splashed with disfiguring grey, her skin had loosened and there were sacks beneath her eyes. Eurystheus noted distastefully how she had gathered everywhere the rubble of years while he himself had remained lean and almost untouched. A loss of teeth seemed to be his solitary blemish; but even this was inward and showed only in the more generous working of his mouth.

The years lay very lightly on Eurystheus, and there were times, as he looked about him and observed the deterioration of everyone else, when he wondered quite seriously whether he'd been blessed with eternal youth. Servants had grown paunchy, dogs had greyed about the muzzle; and as for Heracles—

"He sweats more, don't you think? It makes one feel quite faint. Even time punishes him."

"Not enough! The last Labours. Think, Eurystheus; think of what you dread more than anything. . . ." The queen's sagging face appeared above the lip of the chamber; her smile was as tight and careful as the stitching of a worn sheet. In addition to bloating her somewhat, the years had deepened and matured her dislike for Heracles; and whenever she peered down on the lean, bony and shrunken husband fate had allotted her she disliked the powerful Heracles even more. She sneered at his qualities and belittled his achievements as if, by diminishing him, she was raising Eursytheus to a worthy height.

"Make him crawl, Eurystheus. Make him come to you with his skin in tatters and beg you to let him go. Make him fail. . . ."

"There is," said Eurystheus, tugging a richly whiskered cheek, "something pretentious about success, don't you think?"

Eurystheus was inclined to regard anything that surpassed him as vanity and pretension. Unlike his queen he did not long for improvement; he did not think it either necessary or even possible. His mouth worked tremendously and one by one he

tongued the hollows within. What did he dread more than anything? He had dreaded the Nemean Lion and the Lernian Hydra.
He had shrunk from the filth of Augeias. He had feared the great
Bull of Crete that sired demons and bubbled fire—but Heracles
had subdued it; likewise the nightmarish birds on the Stym-
phalian marshes—brazen-beaked creatures that tore out travellers' eyes, then pecked them to death—Heracles had driven
them away and returned to Mycenae, flushed with triumph.
There had been a boar on Mount Erymanthus that trampled
harvest and harvesters alike, lacing the corn with blood and
screams and bones; there had been a mad king in the east who
kept flesh-eating mares and fed them on men. These terrors too
had fallen before Heracles. The boar had been conquered and
the king fed to his mares. What else was there left for Eurystheus
to dread, save Heracles himself? What was there in the dark of
his mind that came crawling out at night-time and made him
sweat with horror and grief? Death.

"Let him go to the Kingdom of Hades and bring back Cerberus,
the three-headed dog of hell."

"What have you left for the likes of me, Prince Heracles?" asked
Iolaus, half-humorously, half-seriously, as he and his beloved
hero climbed the hilly ground two days' journey to the south of
Mycenae. "You've cleared the world of monsters; and even
supposing there should come another Heracles, what would there
be left for him to do? Hold up the heavens, maybe? Fetch the
golden apples of the Hesperides—or set Prometheus free? Everything else is done. It's a poor outlook for the hopeful heroes of
tomorrow. Not that I'm complaining. At least I'll always be able
to say that I was with Heracles when he fetched the cattle of
King Geryon; I went with Heracles when he seized the golden
girdle of the Amazon Queen. . . ."

"—And to clean the stables of Augeias?" put in Heracles,
somewhat mischievously.

"Ah, yes," said Iolaus thoughtfully. "That was the most
marvellous Labour of them all. No one but Prince Heracles could
have done it."

"Telamon . . . Peleus, perhaps?"

Iolaus shook his head. "Who but Heracles could have shifted

thirty years of dung without so much as once soiling his hands with it? Amazing. Who but the great Prince Heracles could have persuaded two rivers and a boy to do it for him? *My* hands stank for a year afterwards. Perhaps you noticed, Prince Heracles? But of course you did. Don't you remember, you wouldn't take me when you pursued the magical Hind of Ceryneia, because, you said, the creature would have scented me from one end of Arcadia to the other? I'd like to have seen that hind with its antlers like a stag. Perhaps if I'd gone with you, you might have caught it more easily."

"Have you still not forgiven me, Iolaus; and after all these years? I promise you, the smell's gone now. . . ."

Iolaus smiled, and these two, whose friendship had deepened into a many-layered understanding, fell silent for a moment as if in contemplation of some gulf that lay between them, over which, however much they might laugh and chide and remember old times, they could never cross. For long periods this gulf would be forgotten; then some chance remark, some trifling occasion would bring both of them to its edge and they would pause and look across it into each other's unfathomable eyes.

Iolaus, at twenty-one, was slim and swift and strong. He walked as lightly as ever Heracles had done; indeed, all his movements, tricks of holding his head and sudden, serious frowns were copied so exactly from his hero that Heracles sometimes seemed to see his own youth striding by his side. He himself, as the King of Mycenae had noted, had thickened, gained weight and gravity, and lost his earlier fire. He hoped Iolaus had not noticed this too much, and whenever he could he oiled his skin to smooth the rocky muscles down. Sometimes he found himself pretending to have seen something before Iolaus's sharp eyes had spied it; then he blushed to think that the deception might have been detected and he'd exposed an infirmity to a friend.

But to Iolaus there was only one Heracles, and the powerful figure striding on over the painful rocks was as tireless and magnificent as ever.

"Have pity on me, Prince Heracles," panted Iolaus. "I'm not in such a hurry as you are to reach the Kingdom of Hades!"

Heracles paused. His own legs were aching with effort and in his heart of hearts he knew the folly of driving himself beyond mortal endurance as if to deny his own mortality. He frowned, and Iolaus sensed that once again they stood opposing each other at the very edge of the dividing gulf. Heracles held out his hand; Iolaus grasped it, understanding that the gesture was not a bridge but a farewell.

"The fetching of Cerberus is a task for only one, Iolaus."

For a moment the eager child shone in Iolaus's eyes and he looked as if he might have argued the point as he'd done so often in the past. Heracles gazed at him almost pleadingly, and shook his head.

"I will wait for you, Prince Heracles," murmured Iolaus. He guessed that the task from which he was to be excluded was intensely private and important to the man he loved so well. The gulf seemed to widen in a heart-breaking way. "Go now," he went on, striving to keep the sadness out of his voice; "and remember everything you see and do so that you can tell me and no one will ever know that I wasn't with you, Prince Heracles. I want to know everything you felt and thought. I want to know how glorious you were among the dead; I want to be able to boast about you so that, afterwards, when men talk of other heroes, I'll be able to say, 'Ah, but you should have seen Prince Heracles!'"

"How will you remember me best, Iolaus? When I fought the Cretan bull?"

"As you are now, Prince Heracles; at your very greatest, of course."

Heracles smiled gratefully, but reflected—not without guilt—that the memory of Iolaus he'd carry with him would not be of the glowing young man but of the eager, impudent boy with his birthday knife, endlessly plaguing him as he skinned the Nemean lion.

They made their farewells—which were commonplace enough, as farewells always are—and Iolaus returned towards Mycenae while Heracles continued southward towards Taenarus where there was reputed to be a passage into the Kingdom of Hades.

He strode on through the night, endeavouring to put all behind him and fix his thoughts on the task he had been set. He tried to see himself wrestling with the gigantic hound of hell—as if the conflict was already carved in stone; he tried, even, to feel frightened by the prospect before him. But however fiercely he struggled to master his thoughts, he was unable to subdue a creeping host of doubts and fears that had nothing to do with Cerberus.

He feared the weight of years he'd begun to carry, the blunting of his vision and the slowing of his thoughts. Once before he'd met and overcome the God of Death when he'd rescued Alcestis; but that meeting had been in the full excellence of his youth. Now he was to meet that god in his own realm . . . the same god, but a different Heracles.

He swallowed hard and rubbed his hand across his brow. It was not Hades he feared, it was the ghosts in his path and the ghosts behind his back. Would he meet with the children he had murdered? How would they look at him? Would they still bear the hideous injuries his madness had inflicted? Would he be able to hold out his arms to them and beg their love and forgiveness?

These were problems that occupied him mightily and slowed his pace to a dragging stumble. He had almost completed the penance laid on him by the gods; and it was true that the pain of his grief and guilt was now little more than a vague melancholy. But it was still there, and the thought of facing his crime was more horrible and arduous than all the monsters of Eurystheus's mind.

Had the killing of a lion and the Hydra made up for the killing of eight innocent children? Was he really ready to confront what he'd done? If not, then how much more of his life was demanded to set his conscience free? Perhaps it would never be free and all the years he'd laboured were a mockery and a delusion; perhaps punishment itself was meaningless and humble endurance was a vain indulgence that had nothing to do with remorse?

The dawn had not yet broken; sky and land were as dark as Heracles's spirit. He did not know how far he was from Taenarus; he was not even certain of the direction. Presently he came to a wide, slow-flowing river. He could not quite make out the opposing bank, so he rested until the dawn should show him how far he needed to swim.

He was glad of the pause; his whole body ached with the effort of his journey. He smiled wryly. This consequence of age was a punishment visited on all. He could scarcely claim it for himself alone. Even Iolaus would, one day, suffer it—and what had *he* done to deserve it? At that moment he longed acutely for the company of Iolaus and to hear his calmly argumentative voice. How well the lad had grown; how admirable was he in his young manhood!

Suddenly the sound of movement in the water broke in on his thoughts. A boat was approaching, poled along by a gaunt and aged boatman. It was a pathetic craft, patched and tilting and plainly longing to give up the ghost and sink to the river's bottom with a grunt and a sigh.

"Can I ferry you across?" asked the old fellow, spitting in the water as if for luck.

Heracles looked at the boat dubiously. Said the boatman:

"You look a philosopher, my friend. I don't know where you're going, but all ways lead to the Kingdom of Hades in the end. If we sink, you'll get there sooner and may well be spared a more awkward journey."

"But I, at least, want to return."

"Ah, yes, of course. Don't we all?" Again the old man spat and shifted to the extreme edge of his craft to make room for Heracles. "Come sir—it's a fine night for the river."

Heracles smiled and took the old man at his word. Though water rushed in at every seam and poured over the bulwarks, somehow the vessel remained afloat and the old man poled sturdily across the river. When they reached the other bank Heracles leaped ashore and turned, meaning to thank the old boatman and congratulate him on carrying his years so well; but the crazy craft was already out in midstream as if impatient crowds were waiting on its return.

The gloom was still intense and Heracles paused for his eyes to grow accustomed to it. So far as he could make out, the landscape had no distinguishing feature, being flat and extensive. He peered in vain for an horizon and indeed imagined a faintly shining line that rose and fell as if across hills. He began to walk towards it, and the spongy ground muffling his footfalls gave his journey a noiseless, dreamlike quality.

There was a singular silence everywhere—a kind of stretched silence such as sometimes falls on a ship as it nears harbour after a long voyage. Such sounds as there were tended rather to deepen the silence than disperse it, and the distant barking of a dog left emptinesses between each sullen cry.

As he walked on, the shining line he'd taken for the edge of the dawn seemed to diminish until only a speck of silver remained to guide him. He conceived this to be on account of unseen trees rising to obscure his view as he approached them. In support of this, he noticed a scent of cypress—or some such aromatic plant—that suggested he had strayed into a well-kept garden. . . .

He paused; the silver speck he had been making for had begun to increase in size. He frowned. Even though he himself had halted it was still increasing. It was lengthening, filling out. . . .

Heracles notched an arrow in his bow. A man in silver armour stood in his path.

"Do you come from Calydon?"

Though the stranger's aspect was threatening, his voice was soft and trembled with urgency.

"No. My name is Heracles. I come from Mycenae."

"There is a woman in Calydon. Her name is Deianeira. Have you no news of her?"

The stranger was young; his face was almost childish in its anxiety.

"Who are you?"

"Nothing; nobody. But will you go to Calydon and look for Deianeira? She is very lovely, I promise you. But she is so lonely. . . ."

"Who shall I say has sent me? Nothing—nobody? Will she know from that?"

"Her brother . . . say Meleager sent you."

"But Meleager is dead."

The stranger stared at Heracles and hung his head as if in shame.

"I was Meleager once, Heracles. I swear it. I hunted in Calydon with Atalanta by my side. It's true . . . on my oath. Peleus was there, and Jason and Admetus. I killed the great boar. I was a prince and a hero, Heracles; nothing can take that from me. Not all your doubting looks nor dangerous arrows can change the way I was!"

A flicker of pride played across the stranger's bloodless face. "I am a shade, Heracles; a phantom. . . . But I am glorious, Heracles. I am the mighty dead. Nothing can harm us. We are like marble, Heracles, that never crumbles, never decays!"

Such defiance, which should have been hurled in a brazen shout, was uttered in a trembling whisper, for the shade of great Meleager was dwindling away as if in the grip of unseen winds.

Then, when it was almost too late, the phantom laid aside its grandeur and pleaded once more:

"Have you no news of Calydon? Have you seen a woman there, a princess all alone? Deianeira is her name. How is she, Heracles? Give her my love . . . love . . . love. . . ."

The silence flowed back, and far away the dog still barked. Heracles shuddered at the bleak sound. He knew now that the river he'd crossed had been the Styx. He was in the Kingdom of Hades and the dog that barked was Cerberus, the three-headed dog of hell.

The God of the Dead walked in his gardens; a hand's breadth taller than Heracles—as he was a hand's breadth taller than every man—he turned the corners of the strict rectangles so that his robes billowed out like black explosions in the night. Though his countenance was in shadow, there was, at each turn, a sense of watchfulness that brushed the air like cobwebs.

As Heracles waited, he could not keep unseemly thoughts from his mind. There was, he thought, something of the actor about this god—almost a touch of vanity. He found it hard to believe that this was the same terrible figure with which he'd wrestled for Alcestis on the road to Aornum.

He tried to contain a smile that aggravated the corners of his mouth; it was not a smile of merriment, but of relief. . . . No further shades had troubled him; his ghosts were laid. They had forgotten him, even if he had not forgotten them. . . .

"So you would take my dog back to Mycenae?"

An immense time seemed to have passed while Hades paced his walks, brooding on Heracles's request.

"Take him, then, Heracles; but use no weapons . . . only your living hands."

Again the god resumed his pacing, and at every turn made a black surprise.

"He has three heads, Heracles, and you have only two hands. Like all else in this kingdom, he is just beyond your grasp."

The god raised his arm and the dog Cerberus came to his heel. Three heads rose from its massive shoulders and its tail, barbed with iron, lashed from side to side. Balefully it looked up at Heracles, and he recoiled before the huge, unnatural creature that seemed all eyes and teeth. Dog it was, yet appalling in its deformity . . . an affront to nature.

As if sensing Heracles's disgust, the creature snarled from deep in its three black throats.

Which two heads should he seize? All were equally horrible; all furnished with poisoned teeth. . . .

"And then I seized him, Iolaus," thought Heracles quite suddenly to himself. "But how, Prince Heracles? There's not a mark on you—" "Even though he was the hound of Hell, he was still only a dog, Iolaus . . ."

The words danced in his brain. He lifted up his club of wild olive—

"No weapons, Heracles," warned the god, billowing out in stern darkness.

"No weapons, Hades."

Then Heracles threw his club for Cerberus to fetch. At once the monster leaped upon it, snarling and barking; and while its three heads fought among themselves for possession of the club, Heracles seized the creature round its middle and lifted it, snapping and raging in the air.

"Three heads, Lord Hades, are not always better than one!"

But the god of the dead had departed, and Heracles was left in triumph and alone.

15 • The Painted Slave

An old, old man, almost as old as the hills he so laboriously skirted, sat sipping barley wine in a cottage on the outskirts of Tegea. He screwed up his eyes and studied the painted cup from which he drank. He smiled with an ancient amusement. There was a picture on the cup of a lithe and splendid man half-wrestling, half-dancing with a gigantic dog that sported three heads. Similar designs, executed in coloured marble, filled the towns of Sparta and Leuctra through which he'd passed. There had even been men who'd modelled the same event in shells and sand and sat, cross-legged, beside their work, offering eye-witness accounts of Prince Heracles carrying Cerberus, the dog of hell, northward to Mycenae.

The old man sniggered in his wine and the cottager, who'd taken pity on him, frowned angrily. It so happened that he'd painted the cup himself; and he said so.

The storyteller begged pardon; he was too old and poor to risk giving offence. Though he could not have been more than a hop and a skip from his grave, he did not want to be hurried into it, nor leave a sour taste behind.

"He was here, you know," said the cottager. "Heracles himself. He came from Taenarus with the dog of hell. The barking went right through your head. It was like blows from a hammer. Then he went on to Mycenae and stood before the walls, for they wouldn't let him in. They say he stood there for hours, waiting to learn the king's pleasure. I have this from my brother, who saw him. He said the shadows of the dog's heads stretched right up the walls, snapping and tearing so that the battlements looked like bitings out of the stone."

The storyteller nodded. He was stuffed full with tales of Heracles and his Labours; but it was noticeable that it was

always a friend or a brother who'd seen him—never the teller
himself. Well, well, he too did the same sort of thing; nevertheless, all was grist to his mill. He collected the pieces and
strung them together . . . to get himself a supper and a bed
for the night in some faraway mansion where Heracles or
Meleager or Atalanta were still unheard of.

"My brother said the sight was quite amazing. The patience
of Prince Heracles impressed him more than anything. And that's
what I tried to capture in my painting."

The cottager took the cup from the old man's trembling hands
and traced out the profile of Heracles with a surprisingly sensitive forefinger. Then he went on a good deal about his brother
who was the businesslike one of the family and was respected as
being well-to-do. He travelled in pottery which the cottager
painted, and consequently he saw much of the world and its
wonders. Each time he returned to Tegea it was with news of
some fresh marvel for the stay-at-home, artistic cottager to
depict. He'd seen the Cretan Bull and had narrowly escaped
being fed to the man-eating mares of King Diomedes. But never
in all his born days had he seen anything like Prince Heracles,
lashed by Cerberus's iron tail, just standing and waiting on the
pleasure of Eurystheus, the king. "Why! had he released the dog
of hell then and there," said the cottager, musing over his work,
"he would have been free for ever. Mycenae would have been
laid in ruins and its tyrant king destroyed. He was like Prometheus, my brother said; putting up with unimaginable pain when
he might so easily have escaped it. Because we mortals must
never forget that Prometheus might even now be free if he
hadn't warned almighty Zeus about the child Thetis would bear."

"What's that?" said the storyteller sharply. "I know nothing
of that."

"Oh yes," said the cottager knowledgeably, "my brother told
me. There was this prophecy about the child of Thetis being
greater than his father. Somehow or other Prometheus had got
hold of it—though how is a mystery, being chained all the time—
and he knew that if Zeus begot such a child he would be overthrown by it. So it was in his interests to keep quiet about it; for
if Zeus were to be overthrown, he, Prometheus, would certainly
be freed by a new king of heaven."

"And he warned Zeus?" said the storyteller incredulously. "I find that hard to believe. Indeed," he went on in a murmur, staring at the painted cup, "there are many things I find hard to believe."

"My brother said," frowned the cottager reprovingly, "that it happened one summer's night on a shore in Thessaly. It was that part where Thetis comes riding ashore, stark naked on a dolphin. It seems Zeus saw her—and, with respect, you know what almighty Zeus is! He came at her all fire and honey—when Prometheus shouted out and warned him of the danger. My brother said it was only just in time."

"But why should Prometheus warn his enemy?"

"That's exactly what my brother wondered. He wondered the same about Prince Heracles who also could have destroyed his enemy, but never did. One is sometimes puzzled by these great ones and how they look at the world. For my part, I like to think it's because they have more pity than we have . . . or maybe it's because they believe in some deep law that's more important than justice; but my brother, who's nobody's fool, I promise you, thinks that it's because your great men are often simple enough to imagine that because one good turn undoubtedly *deserves* another, it's going to get it. Anyway, Prometheus is still chained to his rock, they say; and Prince Heracles, according to my brother, isn't much better off. My brother was here last month and he said that, if gratitude's on the way, it's travelling on *very* slow feet."

The old man left Tegea; he felt almost personally the cottager's remark about slow feet. In these, the closing years of his long, long life, his feet formed the chief objects of his thoughts and vision. Each ache, each sharp crackling of rheumatic joints, filled him with apprehension that he'd be unable to move on; and the constant sight of his feet—he rarely raised his eyes— sinewy and withered, poking in and out of his ancient ragged gown, gave rise to all manner of conjectures as to why they carried him this way rather than that. Why, for instance, was he trudging eastwards, when the warmth he needed was in the south? Why did he dream of the sea and ships when he was so much better off on dry land?

When he was a child, he'd have said the gods were directing

his steps; when he was a grown man he'd have put it down to Fate. But now, in the hapless clarity of age, he believed in neither Fate nor the gods; he believed in himself alone—all else was a dream. There was no other purpose in his life but to live it out to the last second. In a little while all there'd be left would be a heap of bones and a tangled thread of tales. The tales would be his epitaph, and right to the very end he'd no choice but to trudge onward and tell them. But why eastward, why to the sea?

He reached the coast at Midea and presently was offered a passage on a vessel bound for Smyrna in Lydia. Idly he wondered if he'd live to see land again; lately he'd had presentiments of dying on or near the sea.

Nor was he the only one who wondered; the captain of the galley had similar misgivings. The storyteller looked to him as frail as a dried twig. Nevertheless, Fate, the gods or his own unquenchable will to live preserved him, and when the galley reached Smyrna the old man was still alive. He was even invigorated by the sea air and quite looking forward to telling tales in Lydia where, surely, Atalanta, Meleager and Heracles of Thebes were little more than rumours on the wind.

Omphale was the queen's name—a sumptuous widow in the afternoon of a long prime. Her husband, who had been killed by a wild bull some years previously, had been a paragon of natural excellence; so much so that no man who came after—and many had courted her—could compare, save in small parts. But Omphale, being a generous woman, liked to remember everyone's good qualities; on a short pillar would stand a marble carving of one lover's foot; on a table would be another's hand and wrist she'd particularly admired, while stretched on a couch would be a truly magnificent leg, caught by the artist in a moment of powerful repose. These portions, she'd been willing to grant, had been the equal of the dead king's; but the man who could have matched him altogether had yet to be born.

This dwelling on an impossible ideal, this piecemeal harking back, irritated the storyteller—though he was careful not to show it. It seemed almost a slight on his own imagination which surely stood like a mountain above the mole-hill of this local lady's. Dingy and pathetic though he might have been in person, inside the storyteller's head were glories that outshone life in every particular.

"There was a man," he began, warming his withered shanks by the blazing fire, "who might have matched even your king; but I grant it was a long time ago. And it's possible," he went on, gazing round at the marble items of good men's parts, "that, like you, Queen Omphale, I've collected bits and pieces belonging to many heroes and joined them into an imaginary one. I don't say I have; all I say is that it's possible. Well, lady, this man—if ever he lived—was born in Thebes. . . ."

The queen smiled, half-roguishly, half-warningly—as if to let the storyteller know he must belittle no royal dreams. Nonetheless, she could not resist a story. She settled herself back, one hand beating time to the old man's lyre, and the other feeding sweetened barley cakes to her latest fancy—a painted slave bought off a traveller and whom it amused her to dress in women's clothes.

"Go on, old man. . . ."

So the storyteller sang of Heracles and his Labours, each more marvellous than the last. His worn and cracked voice, rising at times to an eager squeal, presented to the listening queen such a young man that her heart quickened and tears filled her eyes.

Hounded by madness and the enmity of Hera, the young man turned his terrible guilt to such good account that it became a kind of virtue. No task was too great or too menial; the achieving was all.

"Yet this Heracles was ever gentle—"

"Like my husband," whispered the queen, stroking the cheek of the painted slave.

"And this Heracles was kind; he loved old and young alike."

"Even as my husband."

"He had the patience of Prometheus. . . ."

"So did my husband."

"And when at last he was set his last Labour, he bowed his head humbly, even though Eurystheus had demanded the impossible."

"And what was this last impossible Labour?"

"Once upon a time, when the Queen of Heaven was married, Mother Earth gave her a golden apple tree which she planted in her garden between heaven and earth. The Hesperides, daughters of the Titan Atlas, tended it, and there was a guardian dragon, too, that coiled around the tree. 'Fetch me the fruit from this tree,' commanded Eurystheus. 'Bring me back the golden apples of the Hesperides.'

"So Heracles set out from Mycenae and began to scour the world for the Garden of the Hesperides."

"And did he find it—this imaginary garden with its fanciful fruit?" asked the queen. "Tell me, old man."

The storyteller smiled and shook his head. He was too practised to answer yes or no and cut the throat of his own tale.

"One day, by the River Po, he met a man even older than me. This old fellow was sleeping half in and half out of the water. Heracles bent to hold him by the shoulder—for fear he'd slip and drown. But at once the old man turned into a fish and would have swum away had not Heracles held on by a fin. The old man was Nereus, the sea-god. . . ."

"Do you believe in gods, then?" murmured the queen, wiping her plump fingers on the slave's tunic.

"It's no matter what *I* believe, lady," said the storyteller, blinking mistily. "Heracles believed—and so he found. And it was the sea-god who told him where the garden was and how he should obtain the golden apples."

"And where was this remarkable garden?"

"Beyond the Stream of Ocean, where Atlas holds up the heavens."

"And this Heracles of yours really reached it?"

"He reached it, lady; he killed the dragon that guarded the tree and held up the heavens while Atlas fetched the golden apples."

The queen laughed, showing her bright, even teeth.

"Once my husband lifted me in his arms and said he was holding up the heavens, too! Clouds were my hair and stars my eyes. . . . But tell me more, old man," she went on, recollecting herself. "What became of your Heracles when his Labours were done? Did he settle somewhere and raise a family? Did he enjoy his honours as a good man should?"

The storyteller frowned vaguely. The tales of Heracles had petered out at this point. No one spoke of him any further. There were rumours that he'd been gathered up to Olympus to sit with Zeus, his father; and there were darker rumours that the madness had attacked him again and once more he was accursed.

"Well, old man? This hero of yours should have made some

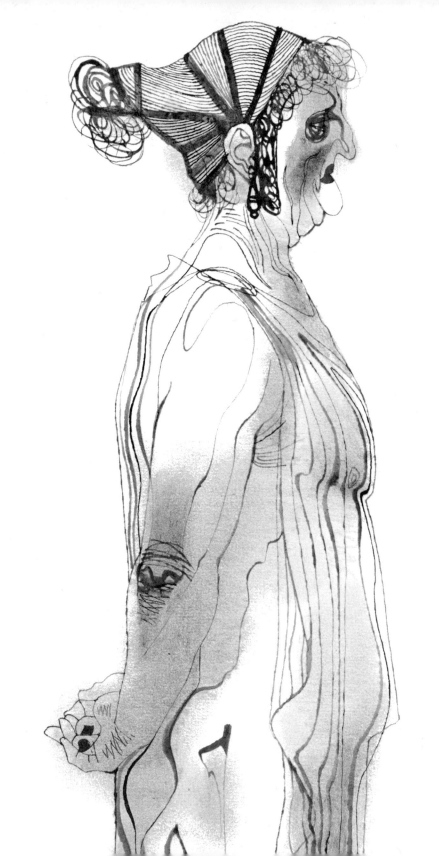

woman a good husband by now. What about the lonely sister of that poor man Meleager? Perhaps he married Deianeira after all and planted a golden apple pip in his garden for an apple tree of his own? Tell me that's what happened; I like happy endings, old man. I don't care to think of your Heracles just lost in the winds of nowhere."

But the storyteller, try as he might, could find no happy ending to satisfy himself or the queen, who proved herself surprisingly critical. He made to begin several times, but his eyes kept meeting those of the pampered, painted slave . . . and all heroic thoughts departed in disgust.

This creature, once muscular but now running to fat, kept moistening his reddened lips and touching his artificially darkened eyes as if the tale of the great hero made him conscious of his own humiliating state.

"There, my pet," said the queen, offering him a cake. "There, my darling ape . . . weep no more for Heracles. Eat, sleep and have happy dreams."

Obediently the slave opened his mouth for the barley cake; and the tears rushed down his rouged cheeks.

The storyteller felt a pang of pity for him, and when he went to bed in the servants' hall, he dreamed of the slave's degraded face in which there seemed to be the ghost of another face, sadly looking out. He found himself wishing he'd never come to Smyrna and awakened with his tale such misery and regret.

"Why did you come, old man?" whispered the slave to himself as he crept from his bed at the feet of the dreaming queen.

He left the chamber carrying a chest in which were his worldly belongings. He slunk across the courtyard and slipped through the ever-open gates, for Omphale feared nothing but that which locks would never keep out.

Once outside he stripped off his women's clothes and plunged his head into a nearby stream so that the paint ran off his face till the water bled with it. Then he opened his chest and took out the ancient, leathery skin of a lion. He wept over it, then carefully put it on and attempted to strike an old attitude . . . the very attitude when he'd confronted the lion whose skin now hung about him like battered wings.

"Father Zeus," he prayed; "let me finish my own story."

Then Heracles set off into the night.

16 • The Gratitude of Zeus

What did the gods still want with him? Why had the ancient
man come so far on feet worn almost to the bone to torment him
with his tales of Heracles in his golden youth? Such a man ought
to have given up wandering; the gods should have left him in
peace; surely he'd earned an easy end.

"Why, Father Zeus—why, when we're no longer hungry,
must you drive us on to earn our daily bread?"

But the cry remained unanswered and Heracles walked on.

"What is there left for the likes of me?" he wondered, wryly
echoing Iolaus's words. He had accomplished the twelve Labours
and so atoned for the murder of his children. He should have
been free. But the hateful madness had pursued him. Though
he'd accomplished more than any man who ever lived—even as
much as a god—the little worm that nested in his head had
brought him tumbling down again. A man had accused him of
theft so, in a sudden rage, he'd killed him . . . flung him from a
cliff. A year in slavery had been his punishment.

It had been a sweet and easy slavery; he'd come to welcome
the humiliation that justly levelled his murderous pride. He'd
have been content to end his days in the perfumed obscurity of
Omphale's court. He was tired, tired of greatness, tired of guilt,
tired of eternal justice.

Surely he was even with the world. What he'd done, he'd paid
for; the murders were wiped out . . . and so too were the Labours.
Willingly he sacrificed the glory of them in exchange for forget-
fulness. By rights his spirit should have been as light as when it
first came into the world. And yet an old man had been dragged
hither to remind him of things he'd earned the right to forget.

The old storyteller's pride in his private Heracles had been
deeply moving . . . and a newer guilt had stirred. Lucklessly

Heracles became aware that he carried the weight of more dreams than his own. What was it Iolaus had said to him? Lift up the heavens? He'd done it. Fetch the golden apples of the Hesperides? He'd fetched them. What then remained? Heracles knew—and sighed; then he turned his weary steps towards the north.

A quiet night, blessedly quiet, in which wounds were healed and longings laid in dreamless sleep. Nothing to fear but the dawn.

Once there had been hopes, but now they were gone, and it was as well. Prometheus the Titan smiled in his icy prison as he reflected that he himself had saved his enemy and so put an end to hoping.

He did not regret it. Soon the dawn would come and with it the iron-beaked vulture to tear at his liver. He knew he would scream with agony; but he knew also that the night would follow and he would have healing peace.

Knowing now that his torment was to be for ever, he withdrew entirely into himself and tried to make a world in his head. This world was to be far fairer than the one his unlucky creatures squabbled over. And the men he'd put into it, this time, would be somewhat less faulty. . . .

The rocks below him gleamed under the stars; the mist of dawn had not yet begun to form. A thousand miles below, it seemed, he saw the sea as calm and motionless as black marble. A speck of silver marked a vessel, with a teased-out thread of wake.

Ever fascinated by little things, Prometheus watched the wake curl and cease. The vessel rested; a pin-point left it and scratched a feathery pathway to the shore.

The immensity of distance made these actions almost impudent; the pin-point, the flea-sized mortal began to nip at the rock with hands and feet too small to be seen. Sometimes it vanished into harsh crevasses, then it would emerge, clinging painfully to edges of ice as sharp as spears. Steadily it was climbing, but already the mists of dawn were forming in hanging lakes of white. For longer periods now the climber was obscured—and only glimpsed briefly as he crawled through the closing rifts of vapour. Once he nearly fell, and Prometheus caught his breath in unwilling dismay. To be so drawn back into a world of pain

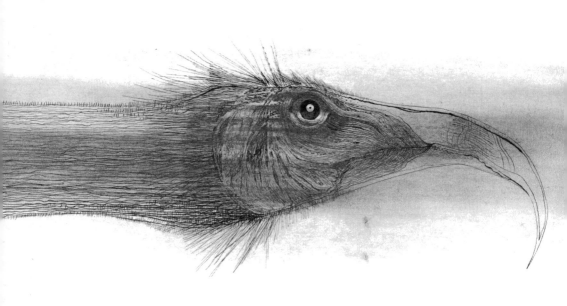

and effort was unkind. Then the climber reappeared on a fragile plateau where he stood upright and waved across the great jagged space of dying darkness to his manacled creator.

Helplessly Prometheus wept to see the tiny, indomitable man greet him; but before he could cry out or return the greeting, he heard the whirring of the vulture's wings. He bowed his head so that he might suffer the first sharp agony unseen by the watching man.

Then he reflected that this foolish hiding of his look of pain would be a betrayal—a weakness before the man who had come so far and climbed so high; so he lifted up his eyes.

The man had strung a bow; an arrow was already notched. Intently the archer watched the vulture's flight, marking each wayward hovering and sudden plunge. Then he shot; the arrow raced like a beam of light and caught the vulture at the summit of a plunge. It entered the creature's eye and pierced its brain, ending it so suddenly that its great wings beat four or five times with residual purpose, before it fell from the air—a tattered ruin.

Then the marvellous archer leaped across the intervening rocks, from peak to peak, as if imbued with the power of the bird he'd killed. He reached the pillar where Prometheus stood and broke the chains that had held the Titan for a thousand years. The gratitude of Zeus had taken a long time in coming; an old, old man had had to travel far to bring it about. But it had come in the end.

A wind sprang up and swept across the Caucasus, sending the early morning mists tumbling across the mountains and here and there letting in streaks of orange and gold. The dead vulture's feathers rustled and creaked, and its ancient head, transfixed by the arrow, tapped and nodded against a rock.

The great event which had occurred was quiet and unseen. No man's heart leaped, no man's dreams were suddenly lightened when Prometheus, maker of mankind, was at last set free.

"Zeus, I thank you," murmured Prometheus.

"It was Heracles who freed you. . . ."

"Should I thank you, too, Heracles?"

"No . . . no. I see it now. If not me, it would have had to be another. Now, at least, I am in credit with the world . . . and grateful for it. It is no little thing to have set Prometheus free. I am proud, Prometheus. Is that wrong?"

"Once I dreamed of a god breaking my chains. But how much richer it makes me that it should have been a man. I too am proud, Heracles. I am proud of my creation."

"Where will you go, Prometheus?"

"There was a garden I had . . . I was a fond gardener, Heracles. Perhaps I'll find that garden. . . .? And you, Heracles, where will you go—you, with your human heart in your lion's skin?"

"I'll seek out my friend Iolaus and tell him that the last task is done. I long to boast a little, Prometheus. . . . I long to see Iolaus's Heracles again. And then—and then I'll find me some glad woman and make her a good husband, as heroes ought. Maybe I'll court Meleager's sister, Deianeira. . . ."

"Come, let's go down."

Together they left the mountain as the morning sun, blazing downward, melted the ice into racing torrents that danced about their feet.

When night came again to the Caucasus, the water froze, jewelling the broken chains and changing the dead vulture into a bird of ice. As the days passed—and then the seasons—the vulture and the chains sank further and further into the growing ice until only fancy could have made out their shape.

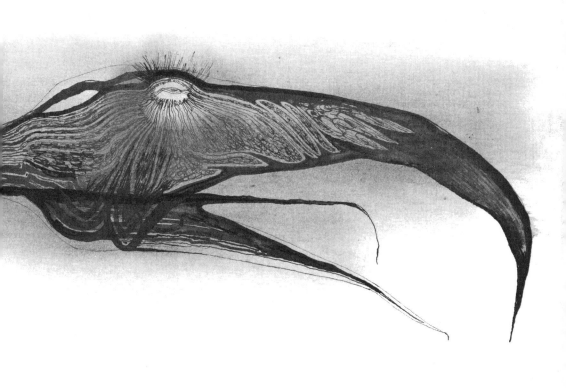

17 • The Prophecy Remembered

Like a dried ghost the old storyteller drifted through the dusty streets of Iolcus.

"He must be a hundred years old," men murmured as he passed. "Just think what wonders he must have seen."

The old man smiled and blinked into the mists that permanently surrounded him; and held out a palm in the vague hope of alms.

"Do you think he's Nereus, the Old Man of the Sea?" children squealed, and clutched at his outstretched hand to see if he'd change into a fish.

Much bewildered, he'd totter round and round, then lean against a wall or pillar where his gown and complexion would so blend with the dust that he'd look like a figure in worn relief.

Yet his brain was still clear—perhaps clearer than it had been for many a year. Whole areas of memory that had once been obscure now were bright as spring water . . . even though the world about him was vague.

He had three teeth left and, on and off, one of them ached. But he knew it couldn't be for much longer and he trusted the faulty tooth would see him out.

Presently he reached the mansion he sought, and fragilely and humorously he was led inside.

"Here, old fellow, here's the fireside; and there, old fellow, sitting there, is the great Peleus you've been asking for. Tell him your stories and maybe he'll give you a bed for the night."

"Or a grave for all his nights," came another voice. "For he looks to me as if he's no more than dust held together with spittle."

The storyteller blinked eagerly, and made out a glittering figure seated in a chair made wonderful by his misty eyes. So this was Peleus, brother of Telamon, the remains of whose robe he still wore. Foolishly he wondered if he ought to draw the great man's attention to the fact. No . . . no, Peleus wouldn't have been interested . . . might even have been angered to see how his cast-offs ended up. For one must always remember that Peleus was the prince who could not bear to be surpassed.

Was it really Peleus, though—Peleus who'd hunted in Calydon, seen Atalanta and even known the mighty Heracles? Helplessly the storyteller gaped, until the draught set his tooth on the hop. He clapped his hand to his jaw, and Peleus laughed.

The sound struck the storyteller as being all too human, and he half wished he'd not made his last journey, but kept Peleus with the rest in his immortal imagination. True, it was a minor irritation, but he'd like to have died with more in his head than three teeth, one of which was bad. He would have liked to preserve *one* illusion. . . .

He plucked at his lyre, though his fingers were grown so leathery he could no longer feel the strings. He began to croak his song of Heracles, much interrupted by phlegm and the senseless giggles of age.

Wearily Peleus listened; he had heard it all so often before. He yawned through the Labours—and the old man saw black holes appearing in his visible world, like little graves. He attempted to sing of the freeing of Prometheus; but his wretched voice failed him, so the event passed in meaningless mumbles and coughs. Then he went on to tell of the death of Heracles.

"In Calydon there dwelt a princess as fair as a summer's day; Deianeira was her name—"

"She was not so fair, my friend; and long past her best. She was Meleager's sister. I knew her well," interrupted Peleus harshly.

"I—I—" stammered the old man, like one caught bewildered in a trespass.

"She was ready for any husband," said Peleus. "Even as Heracles was ready for any wife. Over-ripe, even . . ." He chuckled, and the old man obligingly echoed him.

"But they loved each other?" pleaded the storyteller, desperately clinging to the gold in his tale. "And when Nessus the Centaur tried to carry her off, Heracles shot him with an arrow steeped in the Hydra's blood.

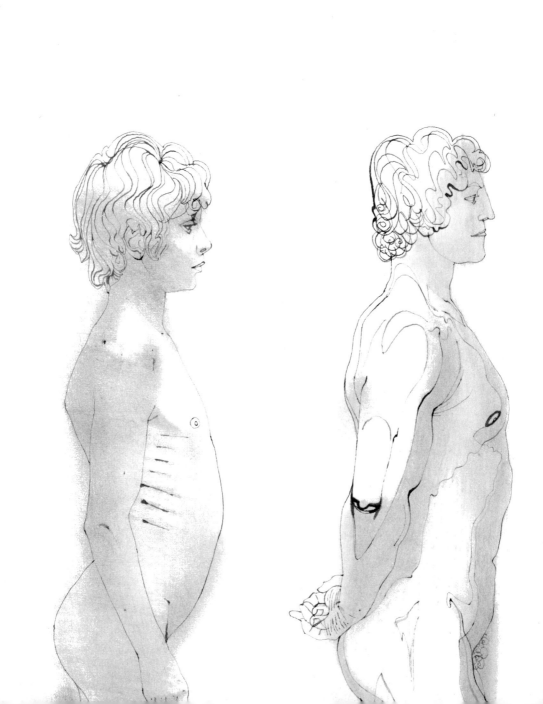

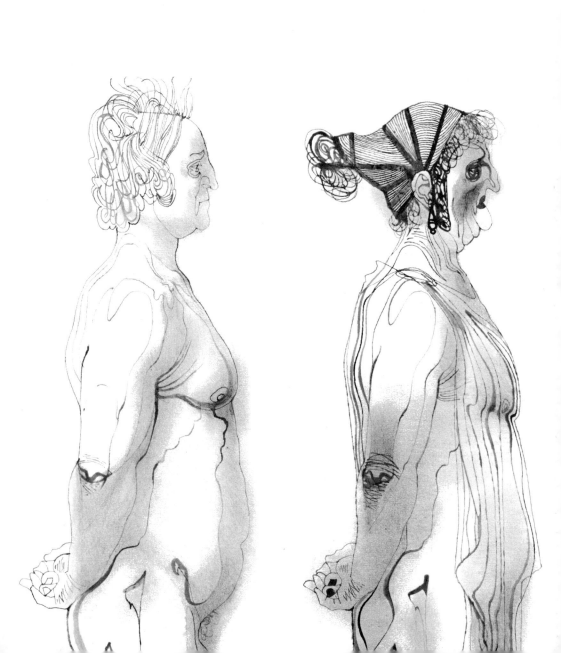

"Now Nessus the Centaur had a shirt . . . or—or was it his blood that had been made all venomous? Or—or—"

The old man faltered. He was getting muddled. Surely centaurs never wore shirts? Yet certainly the shirt of Nessus was important? Ah yes! He remembered! It was the *blood* of Nessus! The dying centaur had told the woman it was a powerful love charm. . . .

The old fellow spat and sniggered helplessly. It wasn't humour, it was age.

"He bade her steep a shirt in his precious blood and if ever her husband's love should cool, then the wearing of the shirt would consume him with passion once more."

"Deianeira was no wiser than she was beautiful," said Peleus grimly. "Like her mother before her."

"Yes indeed! How true! She kept the shirt in an oaken chest even as her mother before her had kept the brand that had secured poor Meleager's life! Do you know the tale of Meleager?"

"I knew Meleager, friend. That is enough."

"Pardon me! I didn't mean to trespass. So—so she kept the brand. . . ."

"That was the mother. We were with the daughter."

"The shirt! The shirt of Nessus, I mean. She kept it to secure her husband's love."

"Love, you call it?"

"Love it was. Heracles was a great lover. . . ."

"Too great for one woman, eh?"

The storyteller giggled obediently; but again it was with age.

"One day in the springtime, he chanced to see a maiden as lovely as the weather. His heart grew young again; he made her verses with his eyes—"

"And forgot Deianeira," said Peleus lightly. "Ah well—no man keeps at furnace heat for ever; and new sparks often shine brighter than the old domestic glow."

"Then Deianeira, like her mother before her, went to her oaken chest and wept over it. She never dreamed she'd have need of a charm to hold her husband's love. She took out the shirt and sent it by a servant to Heracles. He put it on. . . ."

Of a sudden, a rush of tears came into the old man's eyes. His voice bubbled and drowned; all that remained was the bleak, tuneless plucking of his lyre.

"The—the pain was terrible . . ." he mumbled at length. "He—he tried to tear the shirt off. . . . It was stuck to his skin . . . and it burned! He ran and ran—"

The old man was sobbing helplessly as he attempted to sing of the agony of Heracles who had done so much in the world and was now leaving it in torment.

"He screamed! He shouted! He tore up trees from the mountainside! He was dying!"

The storyteller halted. He could not go on. The grandeur of the end escaped him in the pity that preceded it. The funeral pyre built by the dying hero himself . . . the roaring flames . . . and then the final quenching of all his agonies in ashes and smoke . . . all this passed by in a wordless dirge.

"I knew he was dead, old man," said Peleus, after a pause. "But it's a tale I can hear more than once."

He smiled faintly and the storyteller sensed rather than saw that this man was glad of the death of Heracles. Now he, Peleus, had no rival. There was no one who surpassed him.

For a moment the storyteller hated him; then shadows filled his mind. Clouds obscured clear places; he forgot Heracles and he remembered a sea-shore in Thessaly. He began to chuckle as if some enormous joke had just occurred to him. Vainly he tried to imagine what it might be, but shadows kept brushing it to the corners of his mind.

Peleus asked the old man what was delighting him.

"Old men often laugh at nothing," said the storyteller, suddenly cautious. He felt himself to be concerned in some important secret that he must on no account betray.

"Do you know the tale of the fisherman who saw a goddess on a sea-shore and fell in love with her?"

"No," said Peleus, yawning; he was not concerned with the loves of fishermen.

"But it happened so nearby, Prince Peleus. Let me tell you of it. . . ."

The old man's eyes had begun to sparkle; his fingers grew nimbler and a gift for melody suddenly seemed to come back to him. Peleus, about to rise from his seat, was surprised, then bewitched as the storyteller sang in a feeble but sweet voice of Thetis by the sea-shore, asking of the waves and sky, "Who will my lover be?"

He sang of Thetis in the early morning and Thetis in the night-time, sitting on the sands with knees drawn up to her chin, smiling at the sea so that the waves came panting about her feet. He sang of her gossamer gown where the sun came through and showed her loveliness in every particular, so that Peleus's passions were aroused and he marvelled that a man so old could sing of things so young without regret.

Then the storyteller related how Poseidon, Lord of the Sea, came one night in answer to Thetis's longing voice; but he was turned back and the goddess still waited for the lover to come. Then the father of heaven himself—golden-shouldered Zeus—stretched out his arms for Thetis. But even he was not for her. "So still she waits in Thessaly, not very far from here; waits for the lover who, some day, will succeed where even the gods have failed. . . ."

The storyteller paused; he frowned; his memory had failed him again. He knew there was more to the tale, but shadows, golden shadows, kept flicking it to the back of his mind.

"Where is this sea-shore, old man?"

Peleus's eyes were burning. Where the gods had failed, *he* would succeed.

"There are myrtle bushes growing there; and a promontory and a cave. . . . I know it well. I'll show you, Prince Peleus—"

"On your slow feet, old man, even a goddess would have aged by the time you led me there. Farewell, old man—and if you live out the night, make a tale of Prince Peleus, the chosen lover of Thetis, goddess of the sea!"

"Prince! Prince!" cried out the storyteller. "I've not told you all! There was a prophecy! I've remembered now . . . a prophecy about a child—"

But it was too late. Peleus had gone.

"Ah well," sighed the old man, "perhaps it's fitting that the man who could not bear to be surpassed should, in the end, surpass himself."

Then he too left the fireside and turned his feet towards the sea shore in the old, old hope he'd see a wonder before he died.

18 • The Prophecy Fulfilled

She came at noon-tide, riding on a dolphin. Her robe, wet from the sea, embroidered her body rather than covered it. She left her mount, stretched herself and wrung the water out of her hair. She glanced back at the sea, then up to the sun, almost coquettishly. She began to trace a pattern on the wet sand with her sandalled foot, pouting a little when she found a pebble. She hummed a strange, haunting tune and, to amuse herself, danced to it, eyeing her shadow half-curiously, half-amorously, as if it was her partner in the dance.

Then, tiring of the dance, she yawned, stretched herself again and walked towards a clump of myrtle bushes that screened a cave. As she strolled, she swayed her hips in a humorously exaggerated fashion—as if imitating someone she knew well.

"Am I not beautiful?" she murmured. "Am I not worth the risk? What sweeter throne, Zeus, could there be than mine?"

She parted the myrtles and entered the cave. Within it was cool and shadowy; the goddess Thetis lay down on a bed of leaves.

"My lover," she whispered, and lifted up her arms to the empty air. She closed her eyes and her lips parted in a smile; she laughed and stretched wide her legs ... when, from the shadows, Peleus sprang and seized her in his arms!

The goddess opened wide her eyes. Bewilderment, then shame and fury transfixed her. Though in her dreams there had been no clear image of her conqueror, now she was awake she was appalled and enraged by the earthy and impassioned face that bore down on her. Peleus might have been the prince of men, but she, Thetis, was a goddess and expected, nay demanded, a god.

The cave quaked and shook; the cliff above it trembled. Wild sounds filled the sea-shore; shouts, screams, roarings and harsh groans distracted the air and sent the sea-birds flying. Such was the first flush of a goddess's fury in the impious arms of a man.

But in the cave itself was the real heart of the storm as mortal and immortal bit, scratched, twisted and murderously ensnared each other in spells and transformations that rocked the brain.

She changed into a lioness and tore him with her claws. But Peleus held her firm.

"I've known women as fierce!" he panted.

Furiously the goddess turned herself into a serpent and time and again struck him in the back.

"I've known women as treacherous!" cried Peleus; and gripped her still.

Next Thetis turned herself to a blazing twist of fire, blistering Peleus's belly so he roared with pain.

"I've known women as burning!" he groaned; "but I've quenched them!"

So the goddess became water and would have trickled away had not Peleus's huge hands been cupped to catch her.

"And I've known women as quick and furtive!"

Then the water changed most horribly into a huge, slimy cuttle-fish with tentacles that gripped his waist. Suckers reached out and fastened over his mouth as if to stifle him; and the cave was suddenly filled with a stinking brown fluid from the fish's sac . . . a most murderous emission!

"And I've known women who would likewise drown a man with love!" panted Peleus, and held the cuttle-fish ferociously in his arms.

"So many women?" said the goddess abruptly. Her voice was not displeased. "And am I all of them?"

The hateful fish was gone, and the goddess was herself once more.

"Peleus," she murmured, "prince of men. What a son we will have . . . you and I."

Peleus stared down at his goddess, understanding nothing but his victory and not knowing that it contained the seeds of his own defeat. At last, in love and irony, the prophecy of Themis to Thetis on the sea-shore was about to be fulfilled.

Moonlight streaked the sea-shore and lay in a broad rippled pathway across the sea. The night was singularly quiet. Even the wavelets that lapped at the rocky promontory seemed concerned to make no noise and, like virtuous children in a temple, whispered "Ssh . . . ssh . . ."

A figure drifted silently through a cleft in the rock, paused, then slowly moved across the shadowed sand. At last he reached the ruin of a fishing boat whose faded planks gaped as if in wonderment. At what?

Ruefully the storyteller shook his head; as always, he was too late. The myrtle bushes that screened the cave lay in wild confusion as if a tempest had lately passed that way; and the sand nearby was immensely tumbled.

Dimly the old man traced a pattern of footprints till he grew dizzy with the spiralling complications. He fancied some tremendous festivity with extravagant dancing. He sank down beside the boat and set his tired mind to work to make a story. After all, what if he should live another week and have nothing new to tell? He tried to pull his lyre out of his girdle, but his strength was gone. He began to slip sideways until he lay, cradled in the boat's shadow. There seemed little purpose in struggling to rise again. He was going to die.

"It's lonely," he mumbled; "but that's all. . . . Why should I be afraid? Even Heracles died and turned to ash . . . and all his works died with him. In a little while he'll die again and all the gods, stars and mountains will be put out. . . ."

"Will you leave nothing for the likes of me?"

The storyteller opened his eyes. A young man—nightwalker on the sands—stood above him, smiling down. For a moment the old man was frightened; he took the youth for a robber about to knock him on the head. He shrank into his wispy self. The youth laughed—rather heartlessly, the old man thought.

"Great Heracles is on Olympus now," the young man said. "He will not die with you. Hera has embraced him . . . and given him her daughter Hebe for his eternal wife. He walks the halls in his lion skin, and opens the gates for us when we come flying in. . . . Come, old man; come with me. . . ."

"Us? We?" whispered the storyteller. "Who are you?"

The youth stretched out his hand. Suddenly he was silver in the moonlight: his face, eyes, and even the winged sandals that embraced his silver feet.

"I am Hermes the Messenger. Your time has come at last. . . ."

"At last!" breathed the storyteller, and his ancient face broke into the smile that would never end. "A god . . . at last. . . ."